DOES GOD SPEAK TODAY

Also by David Pytches

Come, Holy Spirit

DOES GOD SPEAK TODAY?

David Pytches

HODDER AND STOUGHTON
LONDON SYDNEY AUCKLAND TORONTO

This book is dedicated to
Anderly Hardy of Viña del Mar, Chile,
the kindest of friends to the whole family
during our many happy years in South America

British Library Cataloguing in Publication Data

Pytches, David
  Does God speak today?
  1. Christian doctrine. God. Linguistic aspects
  I. Title
  231

  ISBN 0-340-51092-7

CONTENTS

Acknowledgements   ix
Preface   1
Introduction   5

Part One: Revelations from God

1   A Simple Conversion to Christ   17
2   A Case for Repentance   17
3   A Diagnosis for the Doctor   18
4   A Healed Neck   19
5   A Healed Relationship   21
6   A Healed Arm   21
7   The Right Time to Visit   22
8   Finding a New House   23
9   A Home in North America   24
10 A Home in England   25
11 A Call to Heal   25
12 A Confirmation of a Call from God   27
13 A Good Friday Call   28
14 Just the Right Words of Comfort   29
15 A Call to Write   29
16 Water in Drought   31
17 Identifying a Technical Fault   32
18 A Call from God   33
19 A Call to the Zulus   34
20 An Answer to Prayer   36
21 Prayer-Sight   36
22 A Vision of an X-Ray   37
23 The Face in the Mirror   39
24 A Warning of an Earthquake   41

25 A Warning of an Aircrash   42
26 A Warning of a Flood   43
27 The Cross and the Switchblade   43
28 A Rebuke to a Shoemaker   44
29 A Sack Hidden Under a Mound of Grain   46
30 The Spirit Forbade Him   47
31 'Go to Pará'   48
32 Revival Prayer in Argentina   49
33 God Told Her to Strike   51
34 Tommy Hicks and President Peron   53
35 A Holy Hermit   55
36 What God Thought of Their Worship   55
37 Which House to Visit   56
38 Recognition in a Dangerous Place   57
39 A Four Year Old Boy Prepares to Die   59
40 A Dream Reveals the Hidden Location of a Will   60
41 A Student in Psychiatric Care is Told the
    Duration of His Stay   61
42 A Caller from Hamilton   62
43 The Voice on the Stereo   63
44 A Voice in the Night   64
45 A Vision for a Nativity Play   66
46 A Marriage Made in Heaven   67
47 Does He Believe Now?   70

Part Two: Counterfeit Revelations

48 Twisting Guidance   73
49 Deliberate Deceit   75
50 A Demon That Wasn't There   76
51 A False Prophecy   76
52 Another False Prophecy   77
53 A Misguided 'Word'   77
54 Tragic Disaster   78
55 It Ended in Suicide   78
56 Loss of Faith   79
57 A Case of Confusion   79
58 The Last Word on the Sacraments!   80
59 To What Good Purpose?   81

Contents

60 Self-Delusion 82

61 Zagreb: The Virgin's Blood 83

62 'Panicky Prophets' 83

Postscript: The Need for Discernment 85

Works Mentioned in the Text 100

ACKNOWLEDGEMENTS

I want to express my most sincere appreciation to David Mackinder for yet again helping me with his painstaking scrutiny of my raw manuscript, his practical suggestions and his careful editing, and also to Mrs Gill Skinner for patiently reading through it and sharing her always wise comments which I have had good cause to respect over many years. Any weaknesses that remain (and I am sure there are many) should in no way be attributed to either of these good friends, but simply to the author's persistent stubbornness.

It would be ungracious in the extreme to go to print without noting my gratitude to all those who have publicly shared their experiences of God's revelations to them in one form or another, whether directly or indirectly. I have taken the liberty of rewriting their accounts – but without, it is hoped, losing anything of their essential significance.

David Pytches,
Chorleywood, Hertfordshire,
February 1989

PREFACE

This short book contains a selection of true stories, many of them the testimonies of men and women still living who are well known and respected for their personal integrity and for their work's sake. They show how, acting on what was believed to be a revelation from God, they have been led into all kinds of blessing – from a new birth or the healing of an individual to the revival of multitudes; from the repair of a mechanical failure to repentance for a moral fault; from the silent recognition of an unknown Christian contact in a communist country to the resounding voice of the Lord in a Catholic chapel. Some of the stories have been shared personally and others written up publicly.

Before repeating the testimonies, we list many of the simple ways in which God apparently revealed himself or his will. Readers will decide for themselves, but we believe this random selection from many, many such stories cannot be totally dismissed as indicating merely figments of the imagination or funny coincidences. It surely provides some indication that God is still speaking today in this direct way.

In doing this, God does not add one iota to the fundamentals of the faith once delivered to the saints, but he does provide incidentals to the experience of God which cause both saints and sinners to reflect, and the kingdom of God to be extended.

Specific Examples of God's Revelation

An unconverted man lying in bed at home hears a voice telling him to go to church.

A Christian leader sitting in a plane sees a word written across another passenger's face.

An Anglican clergyman standing by a sick person hears a significant medical term spoken from nowhere.

A minister speaks out prophetically before his congregation to the back condition of a person unknown to him.

A worshipper sitting in church is given the name of a medical condition which is for the nurse beside her.

A vicar's wife is given details in prayer of someone new coming to church.

A vicar sitting in his car is told to visit a parishioner who should have been out.

A lady missionary is given a picture with the answer to a problem thousands of miles away.

A Christian teacher is shown in prayer an unusual detail of a house God intends her to buy.

A nun hears God's voice loud and clear as she meditates in chapel.

An ordinand in South Africa is given a strange picture and an insistent voice.

A retired neurosurgeon hears God's voice during a Good Friday meditation in church which changes the course of his life.

A well-known writer is given the name of a lady she hardly knows to visit in hospital, and is then given an unusual thing to say.

A significant Bible verse is brought to mind in prayer for a certain person.

A technician is shown a mechanical fault before he sees the machine itself.

A dream over a map leads to God's call to unique service.

A comforting revelation to a mother in prayer comes from the engraved writing on a church memorial stone which was not there on a return visit.

A woman sees a picture in a patch of sunlight exactly similar to the X-ray picture of her father's TB-infected lungs which were being sovereignly healed at the same time as her vision.

A man sees reflected in a mirror the last of eight faces he had previously been shown in a vision. The paralysed woman, whose face it was, is later miraculously healed.

A husband and wife separately have a premonition of an aircraft crash.

A dream warning of a flood is followed by three confirmatory prophecies before the flood itself.

A pastor senses God speaking to him as he casually reads a secular magazine.

A preacher is given precise knowledge about a man unknown to him personally in the congregation who is then led to repentance.

A travelling preacher senses the Holy Spirit forbidding him to attend his next engagement.

A preacher is given a revelation about what someone in the congregation is trying to do to oppose his ministry.

A call comes at a prayer meeting to go to an unknown place thousands of miles away.

A vision over a map leads a man to minister on the other side of the world.

A saintly hermit in the desert is given discernment about a visitor.

The number of a house is given in answer to a prayer about where to visit.

A Bible-smuggler in danger recognises 'in the spirit' a man he is supposed to meet.

An old lady recognises in a photograph the faces of people in a foreign land she has been praying for but has never seen.

A child is given the exact date when her parents will buy a new house.

A church is told where to dig for water in a time of serious drought.

A simple peasant ploughing behind his oxen is called to serve God overseas.

A minister's wife is told how to demonstrate to the church what God thinks of their worship.

A foreign theologian having a breakdown is given the exact number of days he will be hospitalised.

A four year old boy obviously prepares for his own un-expected death.

A vice-president of a national bank hears a voice speaking on her stereo which is not there when she plays it again.

Many Chinese miners are saved from being buried alive in an earthquake through the strange impulse of a Christian.

The place of a hidden will is revealed in a dream.

A woman at a revival meeting is persistently told to strike the table but resists. When she finally obeys, the Holy Spirit comes down in power.

Besides these remarkable cases, we have also included some examples of counterfeit revelations to show that this whole area is very much open to tragic exploitation and brings home the pressing need for discernment which we will discuss in the Postscript.

Although we have edited and condensed some of the stories, we have included references where they have appeared in print elsewhere so that interested parties may check them out for themselves. We include a full list of authors and titles at the back of the book.

Those who have been brought up to believe the Bible but to disbelieve that God speaks today may find some cause to wonder, but that should not be so surprising or strange because the whole revelation of God is full of wonder – and so often wonder is the prelude to fresh realities in worship. The shepherds wondering at the heavenly *Gloria in Excelsis Deo* were soon exclaiming: 'Let's go and see.' And next we find them worshipping. Whatever way we are led into it, the focus of all our worship must always be 'Christ and him crucified'.

INTRODUCTION

In 1981 John Wimber, the leader of the Vineyard Christian Fellowship now centred in Anaheim, California, visited England with a team to teach churches how to minister in the power of the Holy Spirit. This was the way he believed God had led him in his own local fellowship, which had grown in numbers during its first four years from some forty people to a membership of over three thousand and has since divided off into many thousands more. He had been invited to St Michael-le-Belfrey, York, by his friend the late Canon David Watson, but on the way he visited St Andrew's Church in Chorleywood, Hertfordshire, for the weekend. It was the Feast of Pentecost as it happened!

He has subsequently stated that the results of that visit made a significant impact on his own ministry. It certainly made one on St Andrew's. For many people present God had moved in a very powerful and beneficial way, and they knew their lives would never be the same again. Other lovely and committed Christian folk were left wondering if it could possibly have been God at all – it certainly was not very like the God they had worshipped faithfully and thought they knew quite well.

Not Really So Strange

However the local church staff seemed of one mind on the matter. There was nothing that had happened that was in any way out of accord with the Acts of the Apostles, and this kind of thing had often happened in church history,

especially during times of revival – thinking particularly of
John Wesley's ministry (1739–1791); the Ulster revival (the
1850s) and the Welsh revival (1904). (Some accounts of
these appear to have been edited later to give the revivals
more 'credibility' to a less charismatic readership.)

Also, what we experienced that weekend was the kind of
thing which was then happening in many places around the
world, and it is still continuing today, following the ministries of such men as Reinhardt Bonnke from Germany,
Gigi Avila from Puerto Rico and Carlos Annacondia from
Argentina, to mention just a few examples.

The Local Leadership Attitude

Because of my own experience of nearly seventeen years in
South America, Bishop Dick Lyth's long experience in East
Africa and the Rev. Barry Kissell's anointed ministry world-
wide (a New Zealander), the staff were probably uniquely
prepared to accept this visitation as God's doing, and we
gave him the glory. There was a relaxed sense of openness to
God to lead the church forward in whatever way he seemed
to indicate, and a readiness to allow time for testing results
long-term – which results have since proved very beneficial.
For example, one elderly lady, who received her sight back
that weekend, has recently died (1988). Her daughter reported that latterly many organs of the lady's body had been
failing, but that her eye-sight had held good through those
last seven years of her life.

Inevitably perhaps, as time has passed, there has been under-
standable concern expressed as more and more churches
of all denominations have set about developing their own
lay ministries in the power of the Holy Spirit, looking to God
for direct revelations in their exercise of the spiritual gifts.

One of the most important lessons that remained with us
from that weekend was the ready recognition that in the
exercise of the gifts of the Spirit there is no infallibility. One
can be wrong, and there is therefore on the one hand a need
for great humility on the part of those who use spiritual gifts

and on the other hand a need for proper discernment on the part of the congregation.

It must be frankly admitted that local church leaders have not always introduced their congregations adequately or wisely to the exercise of these gifts. Some church members have used the guise of direct revelation from God as a cloak simply to express their own whims and wishful thinking. Others have indulged in misguided guessing or – and this particularly applies to those with chips on their shoulders – have abused the opportunity for the exercise of the gifts.

There is always a slightly lunatic fringe in the wake of every new movement who will exploit any opportunity for an ego-trip. There are also some very loving and compassionate Christians who can appear to be quite sure they know God's will in certain areas where angels would fear to tread. They leave their Christian brothers and sisters reverently mystified where in their experience God's thoughts are rarely their thoughts.

It has not escaped the notice of critics that when the late David Watson was dying of cancer he spoke more than once in radio broadcasts of his encouragement from *prophets* (my italics) all around the world who had said to him: 'This sickness is not unto death.' In order to impress upon the reader (who may become enthused by the stories recounted in this book) some of the attendant dangers, we have made a point of including a variety of reported disorders and disasters which have followed on the misuse of the gifts of the Spirit and the failure to seek proper confirmation or submission to discernment.

A Theological Backlash

Some theological backlash is hardly surprising in the whole process of a realistic biblical appraisal of what God seems to be doing in the area of the 'supernatural' around the world today. Some of the backlash may be misplaced, but it should never be ignored. None of us has ever got it all right. We still see through a glass darkly. But the critics have not got it all right either. They also have their personal blind-spots, hang-ups and prejudices.

This was the case when the three-thousand-strong (missionary dominated) Methodists of Chile ejected the Pentecostals in the first decade of this century, believing that the movement was inspired by the devil. Now, eighty years on, when the Methodists in Chile still number about three thousand and the Pentecostals now number around a hundred thousand, people are not quite so sure about which side the devil was really on after all!

Theologians, sociologists and politicians are at last taking Pentecostalism in Chile seriously: see, for example, Fr Ignacio Vergara, sj, *El Protestantismo en Chile* (Santiago: Editorial del Pacifico, 1962), Dr J. B. A. Kessler, Jr, *A Study of the Older Protestant Missions and Churches in Peru and Chile* (Goes, Holland, 1967), and Dr Christian Lalivè d'Epinay, *Haven of the Masses: A Study of the Pentecostal Movement in Chile* (London: Lutterworth Press, 1966). But it took some fifty years before this was to come about.

Early critics were clearly wrong to have down-graded the whole Pentecostal phenomenon. At least one eminent Christian professor of medicine has written dismissively of John Wimber's teaching about healing. We think, however, that he comments with a limited understanding of what John himself is actually saying. The professor attempts to discredit such healing today because during his lifetime some tragic mistakes committed through such ministries have come to his attention. We must humbly acknowledge the truth of some of these charges. We cannot make excuses for them, but only seek to learn from them. But were we to be unkind and turn the same argument back on the medical profession we could cite numerous examples of horrific scandals and tragic mistakes through the ignorance, laziness, innocent oversight or criminal practice of some doctors, nurses and other health practitioners. Would we want to advocate the abolition of the whole range of medical health care services in Britain today on that account? Indeed not!

The following serious and positive evaluations of the role

of the supernatural in 'power' ministries have also recently
come into print: *The Third Wave of the Holy Spirit* (Ann Arbor:
Servant, 1988), by Dr Peter Wagner, the church growth
specialist at Fuller Seminary, Pasadena, California; *When the
Spirit Comes With Power* (London: Hodder & Stoughton,
1989), by Dr John White, the church pastor, university
psychiatrist, popular writer and international teacher
(especially at IVF conferences); *The Fair Face of Evil*
(Basingstoke: Marshall Pickering, 1989), by Nigel Wright,
a historical theology lecturer at Spurgeon's College,
London; *The Gift of Prophecy* (Eastbourne: Kingsway Publications, 1988), by Dr Wayne Grudem, the assistant professor
of systematic theology at Trinity Evangelical Divinity School,
Illinois; and *Healing: Fiction, Fantasy or Fact?* (London:
Hodder & Stoughton, 1989), by Dr David C. Lewis of the
Religious Experience Research Project (at Nottingham University) and the Alister Hardy Research Centre (in Oxford).
These are a beginning, and are all to the good. Besides
them, there are also useful personal testimonies by some
academics included in John Wimber and Kevin Springer
(eds), *Riding the Third Wave* (Basingstoke: Marshall Pickering,
1987) and a wholesome discussion in John Goldingay (ed.),
Signs, Wonders and Healing (Leicester: Inter-Varsity Press,
1989), which is a debate by seven prominent Christians.

Basic Problems

The common feature running through most of these works is
that direct revelations from God appear to be fundamental to
many of the recorded testimonies, ministries and theologies.
This highlights two basic problems:

1 Does God really communicate directly with people today?
2 If he does, then it leaves the door open to all kinds of
   abuses.

There seem to me to be two ways of responding to these
issues.

The first is to set out to prove that God is not doing this today, and to refute or ignore the evidence of what it is claimed God is doing. This was the tactic of the Jewish critics in the case of the man born blind. He himself believed that Jesus had healed him; the Jews did not. Their major problem proved to be the man's own testimony: 'One thing I do know. I was blind but now I can see!' (John 9:25).

The other option is to accept that God does communicate directly with people today and to look for ways of being open to it and of evaluating, weighing and testing it. In our rational Protestant tradition (and here we are in no way seeking to undermine the precious intellectual gifts that God has given us) there is really very little received wisdom on how to do this, and we offer some suggestions about the subject in the Postscript.

Why Bother with Anecdotes?

There may be some help in 'proving' that God still speaks today from the approach adopted by Dr Rex Gardner. In his book *Healing Miracles* (London: Darton, Longman & Todd, 1986) Dr Gardner responds to a criticism often levelled against him because of his appeal to case histories involving apparently supernatural interventions by God. This approach is frequently dismissed derisively for being quite simply anecdotal. Dr Gardner validates the place of anecdotes, even for a rational scientist, by making an observation that comes as quite a surprise for us today. Apparently, until the twentieth century, the corpus of all received medical wisdom was built up on the foundations of anecdotal evidence.

He cites the example of Munro Kerr's book *Operative Obstetrics* (currently in print), which he claims is still a most valuable work for any specialist in that particular field. Kerr liberally sprinkled his original edition with anecdotes, and later editors have added others.

It was Gardner's argument which suggested the value of a book of the kind we now offer.

Biblical Precedents

These 'anecdotes' may not seem so strange when we reflect back to Bible seers who, like Samuel, Elijah and Elisha, could 'see' who was coming to visit and what for (1 Samuel 9:15), 'know' when donkeys had been lost and found (1 Samuel 9:20), 'detect' whispers in the king's bedchamber (2 Kings 6:12), 'discern' the deceit of a covetous servant (2 Kings 5:26) or accurately 'forecast' the end of a long drought (1 Kings 18:41).

Jesus himself manifested such gifts. On two occasions he 'located' large shoals of fish whose presence was hidden from experienced local fishermen (Luke 5:4; John 21:6). Once it was a single fish with a coin in its mouth (Matthew 17:27) which he also 'knew' would be sufficient to pay the temple tax for two. He had personal 'insights' into the lives of Peter (John 1:42), Nathanael (John 1:47), the woman of Samaria (John 4:17–18) and Judas (John 13:26) – he 'knew in his spirit' what was in people and what they were reasoning in their hearts (Mark 2:8).

His followers too also received remarkable 'revelations'. Paul did on the Damascus road (Acts 9:3–6), and so did Ananias, who prayed for him three days later (Acts 9:17). Paul continued to receive such 'revelations' throughout his life and ministry – even to 'knowing' that all the crew on the Malta shipwreck would be brought to shore safely (Acts 27:34). Peter 'recognised' the true identity of Christ revealed to him by God the Father (Matthew 16:16–17), 'discerned' the deception of Ananias and Sapphira (Acts 5:3–4) and 'perceived' in a trance (Acts 10:10) the significance of the visit of the Gentile Cornelius, who himself had also had a vision from the Lord (Acts 10:3).

Positive Theological Reflection Called For

This book does not pretend to offer a theology, but it could possibly inspire others to further theological reflection.

Theology is never static, but is always being up-dated and redefined in the light of fresh understandings of the biblical text and new experiences of God at work today. As Dr Michael Griffiths says about the up-dating of his own critical book *Cinderella and the Betrothal Gifts*, now republished under the title *Serving Grace* (Bromley: MARC Europe, 1986, p. 14): 'That was written seven years ago and has been rewritten . . . *in the light of more recent experience.*' (Italics mine.)

We can only say to would-be theologians that when considering the meaning of 'word of knowledge' it is not very helpful to suggest that by using the Greek word '*logos*' Paul could not have meant 'word' because elsewhere he always intended the word '*logos*' to mean something else. The expression translated 'message of knowledge' in the NIV version (*e.g.* I Corinthians 12:8, and quite variously translated in other versions) is a unique one-off expression, and the '*logos*' part of it is entitled to a unique one-off interpretation in that context. It not necessary that it should always be limited to preaching (which seems to be the position of the much-respected Michael Griffiths in his *Serving Grace*), though it may well include preaching.

In a list such as I Corinthians 12:7–10, it is not forcing matters to look for a spiritual gift which fits with such manifestations as we have already cited from the Bible and the experience of what we see going on round about us in our church life today.

Paul is listing spiritual gifts, and quite clearly each gift must be distinguishable from all the others in some unique way, even though there may be some overlapping with other gifts on some occasions. It is not unreasonable, nor is it any serious violation of the general understanding and sense of the spiritual gifts listed there, to believe that the phrase we translate 'word' or 'message of knowledge' provides the most obvious code-name for that gift which we have already seen operating in the Bible: the spontaneous, supranatural, trans-rational revelation of some fragment of knowledge about a person or a situation which is otherwise unknowable – a feature of many of the case histories included in the next chapters.

Pastoral Concern

The fact that some Christians may be guided clearly and dramatically where for others, even though they desire it, it is not their experience, raises matters of pastoral concern.

There will obviously need to be sympathetic teaching here too. God guides in other ways than by constant direct communication from him – he may guide through a verse of scripture or the church leadership or even simply through circumstances. Ministering in Israel fairly recently to Jewish believers, I was very surprised to find what a common experience it was there to have direct communications from God – even before conversion. It may be partly due to their culture and partly due to personality. It certainly seemed part of their general expectation of God. But God is sovereign and will communicate how, when and where he wants. Those who do not hear voices or see visions, however, should in no way be made to feel devalued – especially when in fact they may be examples to the flock in godliness and good works.

Let God be God

Our objective is not to insist that everyone must be compelled to exercise every spiritual gift, nor to suggest that unless one has experienced God communicating in dreams and visions one must be a second-rate Christian. Not at all. We believe that for generations God has been continuously communicating with his people through prayer, through the scriptures, through the circumstances of everyday situations and through the counsels of godly people.

But we do seek a wider recognition among all biblically orthodox Christians (as we believe ourselves to be) concerning the kind of supernatural revelations we describe in the following pages (some dramatic indeed and some less so; some to well-known Christians and some to little-known ones).

Once there is more familiarity regarding wholesome scriptural guidelines for discernment, we will be in a good position to tackle areas of real confusion. For example over New Age occult influences, which are both heretical and evil, and which deeply concern many sincere and Bible-loving Christians today. There may be some similarities between the experiences recounted in the following pages and those of New Agers. Both may operate through the same spiritual channels, but the spiritual origins and the spiritual objectives are quite distinct – as distinct as between the kingdom of darkness and the kingdom of God.

Part One:
Revelations from God

1 A SIMPLE CONVERSION TO CHRIST

John Bryant from Salisbury, Wiltshire, who runs a firm called 'Cash and Carry Carpet, Ltd', recently shared a testimony at a Full Gospel Business Men's Fellowship dinner. He mentioned a particular Saturday night when his wife Sue asked him to accompany her to church with the children the next day (which was Mothering Sunday and therefore special). Answering somewhat rudely, he said that he intended to have a good lie-in and would not be joining her. However the next morning, while still lying in bed, he heard a voice saying, 'You have got to get to church.' At first he thought it was his wife playing a trick on him, so he just turned over to get back to sleep. Then the voice came again. This time, determined to put an end to the little prank, he put his head under the pillow. But the voice became even louder: 'You have got to get to church.' Finally he got the message, arose, dressed and went to the church. That visit resulted in John Bryant becoming a Christian.

2 A CASE FOR REPENTANCE

John Wimber, who heads up the Vineyard Fellowships fanning out from California, is on record as saying: 'We've had numerous occasions where God has revealed sins of people, either through a word of knowledge or a combination of that and a word of wisdom or prophecy.' Here is an example from his book *Power Evangelism*. He was once on an aeroplane when he turned and looked at a passenger across the aisle and saw the word 'adultery' written over his face in large letters. The letters were of course only perceptible to the spiritual eye. The man caught Wimber staring at him and said, 'What do you want?' Just as he was asking that, a woman's name came clearly into John Wimber's mind and he replied by enquiring of this other passenger if that name meant anything to him. The man's face paled, and he suggested they should talk in some other place.

It was a large plane with a bar, so they went to talk there. On the way the Lord spoke to Wimber again, saying, 'Tell him to turn from his adulterous affair or I am going to take him.' When they got to the bar Wimber told him that God had revealed that he was committing adultery with the woman whose name he had first mentioned and that God would take him if he did not repent. In tears, the man asked what he should do. He repented and received Christ in front of a stewardess and two other passengers at the bar. When he mentioned that the passenger in the seat beside him was his wife, Wimber suggested that the man tell her the entire story, which he did. He was then able to lead his wife to Christ.

3 A DIAGNOSIS FOR THE DOCTOR

A year or two back, I was talking to a neighbouring clergy-man, the Rev. Mike Bell, who related how he had been called to the house of a woman who had been to see her doctor because of profuse bleeding. Apparently the doctor had not taken the haemorrhaging very seriously, and had sent her home to bed with an aspirin. It was at this stage that Mike, as the parish priest, was called in by an anxious husband. Not knowing quite what to do, he prayed silently. As he did so he 'heard' the word 'ectopic'.

To the best of his knowledge he had never heard the word before and did not know what it meant. So he asked the lady if it signified anything to her. 'Yes,' she said, 'it does.' 'Is it good or bad?' asked Mike. 'Bad,' she replied. Within an hour and a half she was in hospital being operated on for an ectopic pregnancy.

Apparently she had already had one such operation, but then it was too late to save the affected fallopian tube. This time the surgeon was into action early enough to save the other one. Had this not been possible, the woman would never have been able to have her own baby. When Mike told me the story the woman had since safely given birth to a child.

Because of my interest in this area I made a point of asking him how he got the word 'ectopic', which had led to such swift and effective treatment for the woman. He said that he 'heard' it, but whether the voice came from behind him or was just in his head he could not say.

4   A HEALED NECK

The following account describes the experiences of a middle-aged nurse who attended a conference on 'Healing in the Church' led by John Wimber at Brighton in 1985, and was reported by Dr David C. Lewis, a researcher for the Alister Hardy Research Centre at Manchester College, Oxford.

He has included the details of this case in a private report entitled 'Words of Knowledge in a Healing Ministry'.

'On the Wednesday night', the nurse wrote, 'I was up in the balcony . . . when suddenly Mr Wimber stepped up to "my" side of the stage and said, "The woman in the cream shirt [me]; I command in the name of Jesus that the arthritis in the third and fourth joints become perfect."'

The nurse, whose condition fitted that description precisely, said later: 'I felt as though I was being grabbed by an unseen hand. I had been so bent forwards shaking, my shoulders had been *so* curved forwards and my back bent, I was almost double. Suddenly I was straightening up, and my shoulders were uncurving. My head was being taken right back, my neck was being forced back and I found myself looking at the ceiling as I could not see anything else! "O Lord, I'm in such pain," I cried. It was agony, and I could not move; every muscle was being pulled and straightened. I felt the Lord say, "This is what I suffered for you," and I just saw him on his cross, bent double for me. Suddenly it stopped; it seemed like I'd been there for ever, and I started to laugh as John Wimber commented, "Another satisfied customer!"'

Her letter was written in November 1986, over a year later. In it she explains how she had suffered since 1972 from cervical spondylosis, a particularly painful form of an arthritic disease. After her detailed account of the experience described above, she added: 'The noise in the back of my head has gone! I'd had a slight crunching noise in my neck for years. I felt as though a donkey had kicked me the next day, and I ached for weeks after. But we have since had the coldest February on record and I have had no trouble. I have *never* had such pain since . . . I have had the odd slightly stiff neck, but I notice it only when I am tired . . . I have had my healing for over a year now, and as a cynical hardened nurse accustomed to dealing with sick people for twenty-three years I would not have accepted this in the past, but now I know that the Lord loves and heals!'

5 A HEALED RELATIONSHIP

We received a letter from a friend who told how, during a church service, she sensed the Lord had given her a word of knowledge for someone suffering from bronchial asthma. Not knowing what this was exactly, and being a visitor to the church, she asked the girl sitting next to her, whom she knew to be a nurse by profession, what the condition was. To her surprise the nurse replied that she did not know, although it later transpired that she actually had the condition herself. She had been reluctant about being prayed for since she had previously had a bad experience of being ministered to by someone who attributed the affliction to a demon.

The nurse then shared that her asthmatic problems had begun following her mother's death. Her father could not cope with grief – neither his own nor hers. He had remarried soon after. Her anger over this had led to a complete breakdown in their relationship. It was then that she developed the first symptoms of bronchial asthma. During the time of ministry she was able to forgive her father. Prayer was made for her healing, and over the following two months this proved effective. The word of knowledge had cut through a barrier of fear, exposed unforgiveness and resulted in physical healing. Four days after the ministry, to her great surprise, she received a letter from her father requesting that they should meet. It was the first communication from him for over three years!

6 A HEALED ARM

A neighbouring vicar's wife, Sue Rivett, tells of a young man seeking the Lord who came to a Sunday morning service recently.

While she had been praying alone early that morning, Sue had felt the Lord telling her that someone would be coming to church with a problem in the right arm, which could not be stretched out properly. The arm also represented a spiritual problem for its owner, who felt unable to reach out to the Lord.

Sue's husband, the vicar, gave out this word of knowledge at the end of the service. A young man who was visiting the church came forward. He knew that no one present could possibly have known that he had had an operation on his arm and was actually experiencing sensations in it at that very moment. He knew it had to be a revelation from God. He received prayer, and the problem with the arm was healed. This was followed by a personal commitment to Christ when the Spirit of the Lord came powerfully upon him. He gave public testimony to this, with the bishop present, at his confirmation in March 1987.

7 THE RIGHT TIME TO VISIT

A vicar, Peter Lawrence, was on his way home at 4.30 p.m. after his pastoral rounds when he found himself driving past Angela's house. He needed to speak to Angela in connection with the youth fellowship of which she was a sixteen year old member. As he looked at his watch he thought how stupid it was to consider calling then, because the girl would not be getting home until five o'clock – her school was on the other side of the city.

He was about to continue past the house when a thought came into his head: 'Go and make a visit; she is there.' 'Don't be silly,' he told himself, 'she does not get home till five.' But the thought persisted: 'Go and visit Angela.' So he stopped the car, thinking that at least there was no one with him to have to explain things to, and there was no one around to see him making such a fool of himself. He would not be late for any planned meeting; he really could not lose. If it was indeed a word from God then she would be there. If she was not – well no one need ever know, and he would go on home! 'Though the logic was flawless,' Peter wrote, 'it was still a struggle to actually get out of the car and go and knock on the door of the house.' When he did so, the door was opened by Angela, who was slightly taken aback. 'How did you know I was going to be here?' she asked. 'I skived off the last lesson at school.' 'God told me,' he replied, trying to look nonchalant.

8   FINDING A NEW HOUSE

Esme Russell, a friend who worked with the South American Missionary Society, had transferred with her husband Paul to Peru after several years of working in Chile. She received a letter from a Christian couple they had trained in Chile asking for prayer as they were looking for a home to rent on a housing estate where they had responsibility for pastoring the church. Accommodation was particularly difficult to find and the need was becoming urgent.

While praying for them Esme saw a large cedar tree in her mind's eye and wrote to them suggesting that they should call on the occupants of any house in close proximity to such a cedar tree on the estate. This they did, and to their great joy found a man who had not yet put his house up for rent but was thinking of doing so.

The house was obviously ideal for what they wanted, and the owner agreed to let them have it at a most reasonable rent.

9   A HOME IN NORTH AMERICA

In his book *Those Controversial Gifts*, George Mallone tells the story of his own frustrating search for a house. An estate agent took him and his wife out to view houses in their neighbourhood to see what was on the market. They very much liked the first little house they viewed, but unfortunately it already had five ready cash offers on it and there seemed no way to get it. No other house they viewed seemed suitable. Their one thought was that if they were to find a house it would have to be by the Lord's help.

A few days later, during the second week of October, their seven year old daughter sensed their discouragement. During the evening meal she looked at her parents and said: 'Don't be discouraged, Daddy, God has told me we will have our house on November the 12th!' As a good evangelical parent, he said he welcomed her optimism but at the same time warned her to be careful about date setting in the name of God and also to watch out about trusting in something which could turn out to be false. However, the next night she returned to the evening meal still convinced. Her father began to ponder these things in his heart (Luke 2:51).

As the weeks went on there seemed to be no time for house-hunting, but as 12 November approached her father began to feel a sense of excitement, though he had not mentioned his daughter's prediction to anyone. When the day finally arrived he 'casually' called the estate agent. 'Did you receive my phone call?' asked the agent. 'What call?' Mallone questioned. The agent then went on to explain that he had tried to phone thirty minutes earlier to say that the little house they had so much wanted had been taken off the market for several weeks because of legal complications and had only just been placed back on again. Immediately Mallone rushed to the house and made an offer which was accepted on the afternoon of 12 November.

10 A HOME IN ENGLAND

Jo Gardner, formerly head of Religious Knowledge in a comprehensive school, has shared in a letter her experience in buying a house. In praying about this she was given a picture of a family of swans on a river, but had no idea what it could mean. When she went to look at the house she was praying about, she was amazed to find that at the end of the garden at the back was a river. And as she walked down the garden she suddenly saw a family of swans on the water. It proved to be just the right place for her, and there were many other bonuses about the purchase of this home in store for her when she moved in.

11 A CALL TO HEAL

Sister Briege McKenna tells her remarkable story in a little book called *Miracles Do Happen*. She herself was healed of crippling arthritis in 1970, and today travels the world taking retreats for Catholic priests, monks and nuns, is sought after for prayer counsel by even presidents and bishops. She ministers healing as she preaches Jesus across the continents to rich and poor alike. She describes how she was called from teaching first graders in Tampa, Florida. By the eve of Pentecost 1971 she was feeling threatened from a growing sense that God might be calling her into something she really did not want to do. She went into the chapel 'to make a Holy Hour for Pentecost'. As she sat there in the oratory she said simply, 'Jesus, here I am.' She had been in the chapel about five minutes when suddenly an extraordinary stillness descended on the place – it was like a cloud, like a fog. A voice said, 'Briege!' She turned to look towards the door because the voice was so clear it sounded as though someone had come into the chapel. No one was there, yet she felt very conscious that someone was present. The voice said to her: 'You have my gift of healing. Go and use it.'

As soon as she heard this, a burning sensation went through her body. She looked at her fingers. It felt as though she had touched a power point. The burning sensation went through her hands and out of them. And then the stillness lifted. A little later she found herself still insisting, 'Jesus, I don't want your gift of healing. Keep it for yourself.' She promised the Lord she would never tell a soul about what had happened.

The next morning she awoke with a voice booming in her head, 'You have my gift of healing: go and use it.' The Lord further confirmed this gift to her through the healing of a child for whom she had prayed that day, though she was not to know the result till later. Then at a conference in California an elderly Episcopal priest prophesied that she had received a gift of healing and that she knew it because the Lord had spoken to her about it in the chapel in Florida. He said, 'Tell me about what happened in the chapel.'

She said to herself, 'How does he know? I never told one single person.' She confessed to him about her reluctance to engage in this ministry, and he encouraged her by saying she was free to choose.

A few days later a woman came up to her and said, 'Sister, I don't know you, but when you went to communion the Lord gave me a picture of you standing with a line of people coming to you. The Lord told me to tell you that you were being called into a healing ministry.' And that's how it all began for Sister Briege.

12 A CONFIRMATION OF A CALL FROM GOD

The Rev. Paul Corrie from Derby relates how God spoke to him during a time of prayer in a house group that he was leading in 1976 in the parish of St John, Wynberg, Cape-town. He was becoming aware at that time that he was to go forward for some theological training prior to full-time minis-try, but he and his wife were very uncertain as to where and how. The house group offered to have a time of prayer for Paul and Lynda, and it was during this time that Paul received/heard the following picture/voice.

Initially there was a very clear picture of a square of blue. (How long all this took Paul could not say . . . perhaps only a matter of seconds.) After a while he realised that the blue square was the view one had if one was to look out through the open sliding doors of the old type cargo planes. A voice said, 'Jump.' But in the picture/dream he had no parachute! The voice was insistent, but at the same time reassuring, and eventually he obeyed (again oblivious to how long in terms of time). However there was no falling when he jumped – just a tremendous sense of being supported and held. It felt warm and comfortable.

The picture was then replaced by another, of a perfect white rose (the sort you would imagine Doulton to make in china – it was beautiful, perfect, translucent). That picture then faded, and soon afterwards, the time of corporate prayer drew to a close.

He shared the picture with a number of people. Some saw the first part as God's provision – of support and guidance for the future. But there was no understanding of the white rose until three years later. Archbishop Bill Burnett had wanted him to train in South Africa, but the ill-health of Paul's father and other factors led them back to the UK and to St John's, Nottingham. After training came a call to a post in Beverley, following a college mission to the place the previous year. It was not exactly what Paul had expected, but it 'seemed' right. Going to Beverley he had assumed that he would be ordained by the Bishop of Hull, having at that time little idea of ecclesiastical workings in the UK. But the service was held in York. And it was there, as he knelt to be ordained before Archbishop Stuart Blanch, that he suddenly observed the white rose on his stole. 'I could have kissed him,' wrote Paul, 'but I managed to contain myself!' Memories of this incident have often helped, he said, especially when things have been difficult or he has been tempted to doubt his calling.

13 A GOOD FRIDAY CALL

One of my former colleagues at St Andrew's, the late Rev. Dr Iain Roberts, a retired neurosurgeon, was at a Good Friday meditation in the church a few years before my appointment here when he 'heard a voice' telling him to rearrange his programme so that he could fit in with any new commitments which the Lord might have for him here. He did just that, and God called him first to be a warden and then to be closely involved with St Andrew's Faith Sharing ministry under the direction of the Rev. Barry Kissell, and later to be ordained at the age of seventy, to serve at St Andrew's for a further seven years.

14 JUST THE RIGHT WORDS OF COMFORT

In her book *Listening to God,* Joyce Huggett tells how from time to time she had been visiting a dying patient in hospital whom she had not previously known very well. There came an afternoon when Joyce could not get this woman out of her mind. 'The voice I was learning to recognise as God's pushed me into visiting her,' she wrote. As she sat by her bedside, holding the dying woman's hand, the same voice whispered, 'Remind her of the hymn, "Just as I am."' Joyce replied: 'But Lord, she's from a high-church tradition. She won't appreciate that hymn.' The answer came, 'Never mind. Quote it.' As Joyce started the first line, she just hoped she would be able to remember the first verse. The whole hymn tumbled out . . . When she had finished the patient gently squeezed a thank you with her weak hand and Joyce left quietly.

A few days later the lady died. Joyce attended her funeral and was startled to find that one of the hymns chosen by the husband was that very one. Later he told her how the words of that hymn had brought his wife such consolation and peace even in the midst of all her suffering during her final pain-racked hours on earth. It was one she had often asked her husband to read to her.

15 A CALL TO WRITE

The Rev. Dr Clifford Hill tells in the preface of his book *Towards the Dawn* how he was called to write it. Early in 1979 he was due to lead a day retreat at the London Bible College

for the staff of British Youth for Christ. The day began with
Bible study led by the Rev. Barry Kissell, of St Andrew's
parish church, Chorleywood. Clifford Hill had never spoken
to Barry in his life before, although he remembered having
seen him a few months earlier, across the room at a com-
mittee meeting.

After the first session they had a coffee break before Hill
was due to speak. 'In the corridor outside the lecture room
Barry stopped me and said, "I've a message for you." I
looked at him in mild surprise, wondering who he knew who
also knew me. I said, "Who's it from?" and he said, "It's
from the Lord."

'I stood rooted to the spot. In the radical social-action
sector of the Church in which I had been educated and had
worked for most of my life, you didn't get messages from
the Lord! Indeed I had always despised those Christians
I had denigrated as having "a hot line to God". I
found myself staring dumbly at him, but Barry continued
unperturbed, "I was at prayer yesterday when you
came into my mind and the Lord gave me a message for
you," he said. "I didn't know I was going to see you today,
so I've written to you." In fact, he said, "I posted it on
the way here this morning. You will get a letter from me
tomorrow."

'"Oh yes," I said dully. "What's the message?" "It's
this," he said, opening his Bible at Habakkuk chapter 2 and
verse 2–3: "Write down clearly what I reveal to you so that
it may be read at a glance. Put it in writing because it is not
yet time for it to come true. But the time is coming quickly
and what I show you will come true. It may seem slow in
coming but wait for it: it will certainly take place and it will
not be long delayed."

'"I don't know what it means," Barry continued, "but
that's the message." I reeled as though receiving a physical
blow in the pit of the stomach, pulled myself together,
stammered my thanks and left him to try to concentrate my
thoughts on leading the day retreat. I have not seen or spoken
to Barry again since then, and up to the time of writing this

preface he still does not know the significance of that message.' That was how Hill's book *Towards the Dawn* came to be born.

16 WATER IN DROUGHT

In his book *Signs and Wonders Today*, the Rev. Dr Peter Wagner recounts the story of the severe drought in the city of Santa Rosa, Guatemala, in Central America. It was 1965. People were leaving the city. Businesses were going bankrupt. Crops were perishing. Animals were dying. Special efforts were made to bring water in, but it was scarce everywhere. Catholics were holding special masses. Evangelicals were holding prayer meetings. There was no rain and no water.

Then it happened. In a small Pentecostal meeting, where some believers from the Principe de Paz churches had assembled for their regular worship service, the Spirit of the Lord moved in a mighty way. There was a message in tongues followed a few moments later by an interpretation. It ran like this: 'Dig a well in the pastor's backyard. There you will find water.' There was much opposition from other churches as the deacons, elders and pastor began to dig. They thought these people were fanatics and/or were hallucinating – especially when they saw that the pastor's backyard was on a hill. A well would never be dug on a hill, as the water runs low. But the pastor, deacons and elders all continued to dig. Soon one of the deacons became quite upset.

'Why is it in the pastor's backyard? Why couldn't it be in mine?' he asked. Another elder thought that maybe the prophecy was biased. One deacon gave up. Another elder left. But there still remained a group ready to press on.

Because of the drought the land was hard, so the digging progressed slowly. On the fourth day they encountered a big boulder. It was so large they thought they had hit solid rock. The disappointments and frustrations were intensified as another elder left the shovelling team.

But they kept digging around the boulder until finally, after two days, they were able to remove it. As they did so, a gush of water came forth. It was rich and plenteous, and they began to drink and drink. It was a remarkable sign for the whole town. What the miracle of the well did to the growth of this church carries on until this day. The number of conversions to Christ was staggering: the entire town was influenced by it. Church membership grew from a few dozen to over nine hundred within that same year.

17 IDENTIFYING A TECHNICAL FAULT

In his slightly humorous book *How to Live Like a King's Kid*, Harold Hill tells a remarkable story concerning the firm he worked for which furnished heavy machinery for a power station in Baltimore. Part of the contract included checking before finally handing it over. One morning he received an urgent phone call: 'At one o'clock this afternoon this power station has to be turned over to the mayor and city council – and it will not function.' They had had the technicians from General Electric and Hill's own firm's technicians working on it for about two weeks, but they were all stumped.

'I began to pray, and immediately while I prayed I knew exactly what was wrong,' writes Hill. 'I saw it as clearly as a picture on a TV screen. This was my first experience with diagnosing a serious and complicated electronic problem strictly by the Holy Spirit.' He says that as he drove down to the power station he was strongly tempted to doubt, but as he walked on to the premises he knew he had been directed by the Lord. 'I walked over to the spot that I had seen in the Spirit as being the trouble source and issued instructions to the technicians as to what to do to cure it. They said, "We've been through all that – we've checked it all out," I said, "You called me in here as a consultant. Are you going to carry out my instructions? If not, I'm going back to the office."'

One of them said, 'Yes, Sir,' although what Hill suggested seemed absurd. They had nothing else to try. 'So they did what I told them, pushed the button, threw the switches and the thing took off like it was supposed to do – to my amazement and theirs.' Hill comments that he never realised till afterwards quite how ridiculous it looked for him to walk on to the scene with twenty highly trained engineers and technicians who had been baffled for weeks and to put his finger on the trouble immediately.

18   A CALL FROM GOD

Jackie Pullinger MBE, whose work among drug addicts in Hong Kong has inspired Christians all over the world, describes her call in the book *Chasing the Dragon*. As a young girl she was praying about what she should do with her life, but seemed to be getting no clear answers. She hoped that perhaps God would guide her by a letter from some person or organisation. But one night, she writes, 'I had a dream in which the family were all crowded round the dining room table looking at a map of Africa. In the middle of the different coloured countries was a pink one. I leaned over to see what it was called. It said "Hong Kong". I did not really believe it but did not want to show my ignorance.

'"Aah," I tried to sound nonchalant, "I never knew Hong Kong was there!" "Yes, of course it is, didn't you know?" said my Aunt Dotty in a superior tone, and I did not dare to argue.' When Jackie woke up she immediately wrote to the Hong Kong Government and then to a missionary society, with frustrating results. She felt she must have misinterpreted her dream. She went out and found a tiny peaceful village church in which to pray. 'Then I saw a vision of a woman holding out her arms beseechingly, as on a refugee poster.' She wondered what she wanted – she looked desperate for something. Was it Christian Aid? Oxfam? 'The words moved past like a television credit: "WHAT CAN YOU GIVE US?" What did I honestly think I could give her? Then it came to me that what she needed was the love of Jesus.' This is the background of Jackie's call to a most effective and inspiring ministry under God within the Walled City of Hong Kong.

19 A CALL TO THE ZULUS

The Rev. Dr Brian Johanson, one-time minister of the City Temple in London, recently showed me the story of his grandfather Karl Johanson's call to missionary service during a period of spiritual revival in Sweden, where he had been born on 10 February 1868.

As a young farmer's boy Karl was out ploughing one day, with the oxen moving along steadily before him, when he felt himself to be suddenly surrounded with a heavenly atmosphere. 'I thought of stopping the oxen,' he wrote, 'but I could not utter a word.' An unseen hand seemed to touch him, and he heard (whether with the inner or the outer ear, he said he could not tell) a clear voice saying: 'Will you go as my messenger to Africa?' The one who spoke waited for a reply. 'My whole being trembled and I longed to run home to my employer, who was a Christian farmer, but I knew that a personal reply was required of me,' he wrote. 'I then answered with fear and trembling: "Yes, if you yourself will go with me." At once the voice replied: "I will never leave you or forsake you." With that the heavenly presence withdrew as suddenly as he had appeared.'

His account continues: 'It is impossible to describe the situation I found myself in, and the turmoil of my heart.' He knew his family would not understand. The call was so sacred he could share it with very few people. 'My life's plans crashed around me. I had a call to go to Africa, but knew of no organisation through which I could go. Severe temptations from the evil one beset me. I thought at times that my mind would give way. Doubts concerning the existence of God and the truth of the Bible overwhelmed me like a flood. All that I had learned, heard and read was scattered like straw before the wind.'

But the fact of his call remained steadfast throughout. Karl Johanson went out to South Africa under the Swedish Holiness Union in 1893. He remained there (with his Norwegian wife, whom he met there, and their family) serving the Lord faithfully for many, many years as the director of the Swedish Zulu Mission, until he was 'called home' on 1 October 1945, loved and respected by all.

20 AN ANSWER TO PRAYER ('HOW LONG WILL HE LIVE, LORD?')

In her moving book *William's Story*, Rosemary Attlee tells of her anguish as she wrestled with the fact that her seventeen year old son William was dying of leukaemia. While her family were off shopping she went into the quiet, little-used (and soon to be closed) St Peter's Church, Sandwich. There she desperately implored God to let her know the time-span of William's illness.

'In an instant there seemed to be an agreement,' she writes. 'If I happened to be standing on a memorial stone I could read that as a sign.' Slowly she looked down to a nineteenth-century inscription at her feet. The stone commemorated a man who had died aged twenty and a few weeks. Rosemary took that to be God's answer. And so it turned out to be: William died aged twenty plus a few weeks.

When she later revisited the same church with her husband to look at the stone once again, they searched the whole floor, *but there was no stone.* Clearly God had given her a word of knowledge through a vision similar to the inscription on the wall of King Belshazzar's banqueting hall (Daniel 5:25).

21 PRAYER-SIGHT

From an article in the magazine of the Africa Inland Mission International, we learn that the Lord showed a lady in prayer the faces of the people overseas whom she prayed for, and that when later shown their photographs she was able to recognise them.

A missionary had written from Kenya to an elderly lady back home in Scotland, asking her to pray for the children in the baby-care home where she worked. When the time came for her to return to Scotland for a period of leave she even wondered if the old lady would actually recognise her.

'Not only did she recognise me, she also recognised the pictures in the photograph album. "Ah, there's Chepkemoi and there's Kendu – and dear little Kiprotich," she murmured happily.' 'But how can you tell that?' the missionary marvelled. It was the first time she had ever set eyes on pictures of these people, and there were no names in the album.

She looked at the nurse with the matter-of-fact simplicity of those who, in the tradition of Brother Lawrence, continually practise the presence of God, and explained: 'God showed me their faces as I prayed.'

22   A VISION OF AN X-RAY

In her well-known book *Something More*, Catherine Marshall tells a story about her friend Virginia and her sixty-three year old father Roy Wolft, who had been diagnosed as suffering from TB. Virginia's father had been admitted to the Tampa Tuberculosis Sanatorium seven months previously, after an X-ray had revealed three cavities, each about the size of a silver dollar, in the top of his left lung. He was not responding to treatment, and his health was in serious decline.

The hospital was treating Mr Wolft with INH (Isoniazid), which was considered a miracle drug, but it was doing nothing for him. Two cavities had enlarged into what looked like a figure of eight. His doctor dared not prescribe the drug for longer than another six weeks. There seemed little hope.

One day, some three weeks later, Virginia was reclining across her bed, after meditating on her Bible, and turned her head to one side to take a nap. Her eye was attracted towards a patch of sunlight on the wall. She was still following the train of her meditation when she was interrupted by the vision of an X-ray picture of lungs, three times larger than life, which was coming into focus in the middle of the sunlit patch. She was convinced that this was an enlarged replica of the X-ray of her father's lung. She recognised that unusual figure-of-eight cavity and the other silver dollar-sized one at the top of the left lung. She had studied these same shadows and scar tissues so often on the hospital X-rays.

Still puzzling over whatever the vision could mean, she saw a white line about three inches wide move slowly up the wall. As the white line passed the lower tissues of the lung, it left behind healthy lungs with the scar tissue gone. It continued moving over the diseased parts, and she observed now that all the tissues were healed, with no more cavities. Virginia stared at the vision, not knowing what to make of it. She had not been thinking of her father, much less praying for him. Then to her amazement she saw a replay of the whole scene on the wall – exactly as before, leaving behind two perfect lungs. 'Then Dad's well,' she whispered to herself. She immediately phoned her mother to tell her the news, 'Mother, Dad's healed,' she insisted. Her mother tried to calm her down, feeling sure that Virginia was out of her mind.

A few days later fresh X-rays were taken as part of the normal procedure. Virginia now had very special reasons for wanting to know the results, but they were slow in coming as the hospital reported that there had been a muddle-up. They claimed that they had been sent X-ray pictures of someone who had clearly never had TB. As by now the reader can imagine, the next X-rays not only revealed no sign of TB at all but the sputum and culture tests were also negative. 'How do you explain that?' Virginia asked the doctor. 'I haven't

any explanation,' he admitted. Then Virginia went with the
doctor to see her father and they were able to hear his side of
the story.

'It happened one day at my nap time. I was just lying
here,' he said, 'when all at once there was the strangest
feeling – like something draining from my body and out of my
feet. A surge of well-being then filled my whole body. I felt
warm and cared for and loved – loved, that's it. Loved! Never
felt so well in my life! No reason to be here now! I'm going
home.' On comparing notes, it turned out that Mr Wolft's
healing came at the same time that Virginia was receiving
that revelation of the picture in the sunlit patch.

23   THE FACE IN THE MIRROR

A young Sri Lankan Bible student was giving himself to long
hours of prayer when he felt an unusual movement of God's
Spirit. His eyes fell on the mirror, upon which he saw an
arrangement of unfamiliar faces looking back at him. The
student, Colton Wickramaratne, stared back at the faces – all
clearly belonging to Westerners except for one, a beautiful
Asian girl. As he reflected upon whatever the meaning of this
strange vision could be, he sensed God speaking to him:
'These eight people will touch Asia with the gospel. These
eight people will be instrumental in a great Asian revival to
come.' The Lord then told Colton that he would meet each of
these eight people, but that he was not to tell anyone what he
had seen until he had met the eighth and final person. The
vision and the message left such a deep and ineradicable
impression on the young man that he could never forget it.

As the years went by he met seven of the faces one by one,

but the last still eluded him, until finally he recognised her in the most surprising way. He had been visiting a Christian girl in hospital who was almost paralysed due to a fall when she was a university undergraduate. The visit, he felt, had been rather unsatisfactory, and he was returning to his car outside when he happened to glance up at the window of the ward the paralysed patient was in. There it was! Reflected in the mirror of her room he saw the eighth face – that of the Asian girl!

He returned at once to her ward, only to find it a most inconvenient moment; the girl was passing through a spasm of extreme pain. She seemed unimpressed when he told her that God was going to heal her and make her a witness in Asia. Nearly a year later, this same girl, still paralysed and stretched out upon her bed, suddenly heard what sounded like a man's voice. 'Mita,' it said, 'I'm going to raise you up to make you a witness in Asia.' She could hardly believe her ears. Someone was surely playing a trick on her. Then she heard a further word, 'I'm going to heal you on Friday, the 11th of February.' The 'voice' seemed to have come from behind her back. She could neither see nor sense anyone. Mita had never been impressed by people who claimed to have heard from God. It made her very suspicious of them, but deep in her heart she knew that this had to be God.

Later at Colton's church, where Mita had been taken in a wheelchair, a 'tongue' was given, the interpretation of which confirmed the earlier promise to her. It ran: 'God will raise you up to be a witness to all Asia. His word to you is true. Trust him. He will not lead you astray. He will glorify himself through you.' She knew now that God had spoken to her, but still she shared it with no one.

Back at the hospital she reflected upon it and prayed: 'Father, you have told me the day and the date. Please don't keep me waiting all day! Please tell me the time too.' She half expected to hear the 'voice' again, but instead she sensed in her heart that God had appointed for it to happen at 3.30 p.m. in the afternoon of Friday 11 February.

Once again – this time as she lay back in a chair for the

disabled at church the following week – God's word was confirmed. Mita has the documented evidence that she was completely paralysed for a year. Soon after that last church service, Colton, her pastor, went to see her. He seemed to know something too. 'What has God told you?' he asked. He read her lips (by now she could not even speak), and she told him about the time for the promised healing. It was planned to invite a number of believers to her room on Friday 11 February – among them were two Christian doctors.

It was to the minute exactly that complete healing came to Mita. She was literally catapulted from her chair as the power of God came upon her for her healing. This amazing story is told fully by Mita herself and Mark Buntain in the book *Miracle in the Mirror*, and is attested by such a well-known Christian as Brother Andrew.

24 A WARNING OF AN EARTHQUAKE

Dr Peter Wagner, in his *Signs and Wonders Today*, attempts to find some explanation for the amazing growth of the church in China during the Cultural Revolution which began in 1949 after Chairman Mao Tse-tung had expelled all missionaries and liquidated (or exiled to labour camps) all the national church leadership. There were many martyrs, only limited fellowship, and no Bibles. Wagner believed that 'signs and wonders' played a major role in this church growth. He relates the case of one woman who had worked at a quarry in charge of the work shifts. When she blew a whistle, the workers would come up out of the mines.

One day she was working in her office when she heard a voice calling her by name, telling her that she should blow the whistle to let the workers come up out of the mines. There was still another hour before she was supposed to do this, but she repeatedly heard the voice telling her to blow her whistle now. Finally, without checking with the other members of the office because she feared they would stop her, she blew the whistle. The miners started coming out. No sooner had the last one left the mines than an earthquake caved in several of the shafts. If the workers had still been in the mines, the death toll would have been staggering.

The miners gathered round this girl and asked why she had blown the whistle early. She had to admit that she was a Christian and that she had just obeyed the voice of God. Hundreds accepted the Lord that day. Then, at an official enquiry, she gave a powerful testimony and many more families accepted Christ.

25   A WARNING OF AN AIRCRASH

In his book *The Cost of Commitment*, Dr John White, a widely-travelled Christian psychiatrist and a well-known writer, tells of what he calls a premonition of danger for his wife and family when they were flying off to Bolivia on an alternative route to his own. He felt too foolish to tell her, and went through agonies after he left her. After a tremendous struggle in prayer he felt quite clearly that God was saying: 'Trust me.' The plane crashed. Everyone on board was killed. It was a terrible disaster. But his wife had also experienced a premonition, and had cut the journey short – she never reboarded the plane for the last take-off before the tragedy occurred.

26   A WARNING OF A FLOOD

Jack Coe, who died young, was an evangelist born in 1918. In
one campaign he saw as many as thirty thousand people
come to Christ. George Canty, in his book *The Practice of
Pentecost*, tells how Coe had a dream one day in which he saw
a flood. The dream troubled him, and he told it to his wife.
Later, when he was in Kansas City, God began to speak
through the gift of prophecy, saying that if the people would
not repent a judgement would come upon them. Three
similar prophecies were uttered. Once again Coe dreamed
about the flood, which made him feel that he was meant to
move his ten thousand seater tent. Then God spoke clearly
and told him to go, and he started packing up. The last hours
of the removal were sheer panic, and many unbelievers
mocked as Coe and his helpers fled in their loaded trucks.
They were only just in time. The river rose twenty-two feet,
and the ensuing flood brought the worst disaster of its kind in
North American history.

27   THE CROSS AND THE
SWITCHBLADE

Those who have read David Wilkerson's bestseller *The Cross
and the Switchblade* will remember how God first called him to
a ministry among New York's teenage street gangs. He was
just a country-bumpkin preacher, ministering in a farming
community at the time. He had never actually been to New
York before, and was simply sitting in his rural home one

evening reading *Life* magazine when his attention was drawn
to an artist's picture of bewilderment, hatred and despair in
the eyes of one of seven boys on trial for the brutal murder of a
fifteen year old polio victim. Wilkerson was revolted, and he
found himself crying involuntarily. But the thought suddenly
came to him, 'Go to New York and help those boys.' He
quickly dismissed it as ridiculous. But there it was again: 'Go
to New York and help those boys.' The thought became vivid
and persistent and seemed to be completely independent of
his own feelings and ideas. 'I'd be a fool,' he rationalised. 'I
know nothing about kids like that. I don't even want to
know.' It was no use. The idea would not go away. He
resolved to go to New York! He tells the story of what
followed in a book which is full of daring, excitement,
hardship and miracles – a book which, incidentally, played a
singular role in the beginnings of renewal within the Catholic
Church of the USA. *The Cross and the Switchblade* shows how
Wilkerson's obedience to God's call changed the course of
many, many lives, including his own.

28 A REBUKE TO A SHOEMAKER

In *The Early Years*, the first volume of his autobiography, the
famous nineteenth-century Baptist preacher C. H. Spurgeon
tells the following story.

'There were many instances of remarkable conversions at
the Music Hall: one especially was so singular that I have
often related it as proof that God sometimes guides his
servants to say what they themselves would never have
thought of uttering, in order that he may bless the hearer for
whom the message is personally intended.

'While preaching in the hall on one occasion, I deliberately pointed to a man in the midst of the crowd and said, "There is a man sitting there, who is a shoemaker; he keeps his shop open on Sundays. It was open last Sabbath morning; he took ninepence and there was fourpence profit out of it. His soul is sold to Satan for fourpence!"

'A city missionary, when going on his rounds, met with the man and seeing that he was reading one of my sermons, he asked the question, "Do you know Mr Spurgeon?" "Yes," replied the man, "I have every reason to know him. I have been to hear him, and, in his preaching, by God's grace I have become a new creature in Christ Jesus. Shall I tell you how it happened? I went to the Music Hall and took my seat in the middle of the place; Mr Spurgeon looked at me as if he knew me, and in his sermon he pointed to me and told the congregation that I was a shoemaker and that I kept my shop open on Sundays; and I did sir. I should not have minded that, but he also said that I took ninepence the Sunday before, and that there was fourpence profit out of it. I did take ninepence the Sunday before, and there was fourpence profit out of it, but how he should know that I could not tell. Then it struck me that it was God who had spoken to my soul through him, so I shut up my shop the next Sunday. At first I was afraid to go again to hear him, lest he should tell the people more about me, but afterwards I went and the Lord met with me and saved my soul."'

Spurgeon reckoned he could tell of as many as a dozen similar cases in which he had pointed to someone in the hall without having the slightest knowledge of the person, or any idea that what he said was right, except that he was moved by the Spirit to say it. 'So striking have been my descriptions,' he said, 'that the persons have gone away, and said to their friends, "Come, see a man that told me all things that ever I did; beyond any doubt he must have been sent of God to my soul, or else he could not have described me so exactly."'

That was not all that Spurgeon had to say on the subject: 'I have known many instances in which the thoughts of men have been revealed from the pulpit. I have sometimes seen

persons nudge their neighbours with their elbow, because
they had got a smart hit, and they have been heard to say,
when they were going out, "The preacher told us just what
we said to one another when we went in at the door."'

29 A SACK HIDDEN UNDER A MOUND OF GRAIN

News arrived in 1900 that a party of some hundred Russian
Christians in covered wagons was coming down to Armenia
from the mountains. These were Russian-Orthodox-
Christians-turned-Pentecostalists who were arriving at the
village where Demos Shakarian had his farm. Demos insisted
upon a welcoming feast for them in the yard by his farmhouse
and went out to select the fattest steer from his herd for the
celebration. But the steer he chose was blind in one eye.

Now Demos, who came from a Presbyterian tradition, still
observed to the letter certain Old Testament laws and
believed that according to ceremonial law (Leviticus 22:20)
the steer, being blemished, was unacceptable as a sacrifice to
the Lord. But he silenced his conscience on the grounds that
it was the fattest steer there, and he proceeded to butcher the
beast in the barn. He hid the head with the offending eye in a
sack beneath a pile of grain.

As the evening drew in, all the guests assembled around
long plank tables waiting for the food to be blessed. These
Russian Christians would never pray, not even give thanks
for food, without waiting first for what they called 'the
anointing' – expecting the Holy Spirit to fall upon them.
They claimed they could feel his presence.

When this happened round the table in the farmyard that
evening, an old patriarch at the party raised his hand – not to

bless the food, but to indicate a hold-up in the proceedings. He then strode across the yard into the barn, only to reappear a moment later with the sack that he had retrieved from under the grain. As he put it down the sacking fell away, revealing the blind eye in the severed head of the steer.

'Have you anything to confess, Brother Demos?' the Russian demanded. 'Yes, I have,' admitted Demos. 'But how did you know?' (The Russians had not even entered the village when Demos was butchering the steer!) 'God told me,' the patriarch replied simply. 'You still do not believe that God speaks to his people today as in the past. The Spirit gave me this word of knowledge for a reason: that you and your family might believe. You have been resisting the power of the Holy Spirit. Today is the day when you will resist no longer.' And it was so.

Demos Shakarian began to learn to walk in the Spirit, and this led to his eventually emigrating to California in 1905, heeding a prophetic warning which was horrifically fulfilled in 1914 when the Armenians were massacred by the Turks. That word of knowledge not only changed the course of his life but, inevitably, that of his family. In 1957 his grandson, also called Demos, founded the 'Full Gospel Business Men's Fellowship International', which now has thousands of chapters around the world, reaching more than a billion people a year with the gospel. His story is told in his *The Happiest People on Earth*.

30 THE SPIRIT FORBADE HIM

In his book on *The Welsh Revival of 1904*, Eifion Evans records how Evan Roberts operated through revelations which he believed he received from God. 'His acceptance or refusal of

the pressing invitations he received were determined solely
on the basis of the Spirit's constraint . . . His proposed visit to
Cardiff, for instance, was suddenly postponed indefinitely
because he sensed the Spirit of God forbidding him to go.'

Evan Roberts, who had influence right across the world,
frequently received these words of knowledge. He visited
Liverpool from Wales in 1905. At his first meeting he publicly named in person disobedient men and scoffers present at
the meetings. On one occasion in the Sun Hall, a packed
building accommodating six thousand people, Roberts
stopped the service and announced in Welsh and English
that there was an Englishman at the meeting who was trying
to hypnotise him at that very moment. He called on him to
leave the hall at once and seek the Lord's forgiveness: 'God
will not be mocked. We do not come here to play. We come
here to worship the Lord . . .' The truth of that assertion was
later acknowledged publicly by a hypnotist appearing at the
Lyric Theatre.

31   'GO TO PARÁ'

The Assemblies of God Church is the largest Protestant
denomination in Brazil, today numbering well over ten
million members. The Church was born out of a direct
revelation from God. In 1909 two Swedish immigrants in the
USA, Gunnar Vingren and Daniel Berg, were attending a
small prayer meeting at South Bend, Indiana, where they
received a prophecy telling them to go to Pará – a place they
had never heard of and had no idea where to look for on the
map.

Going to the public library, they discovered there was a

state by that name in Brazil. Another prophecy came later,
telling them to go to New York to look for a certain man at a
certain place, and although they barely had sufficient cash
they went and found the man, as had been predicted. He
gave them the exact amount of money needed for two
third-class passages on a freighter to the city of Belém – the
capital of Pará.

They eventually arrived there in 1910, most inappro-
priately attired for a tropical city. After prayer they were led
to a Methodist missionary who introduced them to a Baptist
pastor. He befriended them and found lodgings for them on
the church premises. All went well from then on until they
became reasonably proficient in Portuguese. Then serious
trouble arose between them. This was over the substance of
their preaching, which, being too Pentecostal, was deemed
unacceptable to the Baptist Church. They finally had to
leave, and formed a new congregation which became known
as the Assemblies of God in Brazil. Today the Belém Church
itself numbers over thirty thousand, including a ring of
daughter churches in the immediate vicinity. By 1984 the
number of people in the Assemblies of God Church in Brazil
had grown to nine million.

32   REVIVAL PRAYER IN ARGENTINA

In his book *Cry For Me Argentina*, Dr R. E. Miller shares
something of the prayer which preceded the revival that
centred on Tommy Hicks in 1952. He writes of that which he
knows personally, though he believes there were many other
groups praying for revival up to that time.

One account he gives is of extraordinary stirrings in the
Bible Training Institute in the little town of City Bell, just
outside Buenos Aires, on 4 June 1951. Alexander, a teenager
of Polish descent, down from the Chaco, was still in prayer
long after midnight when he sensed a strange feeling of
something pressing down upon him, an intense great light
surrounding him and a heavenly being enfolding him. The
boy was terrified and fled back to the Institute.

The heavenly visitor entered the Institute with him, and in
a few moments all the students were awake with the fear of
God upon them. They began to cry out in repentance as God
by his Spirit dealt with them. The next day the Spirit of God
came again upon Alexander as he was given prophecies
of God's moving in far off countries. The following day,
Alexander again saw the Lord in the Spirit, but this time he
began to speak slowly and distinctly the words he heard from
the angel of God. No one could understand what he was
saying, however, until another lad named Celsio (with even
less education than Alexander), overcome with the Spirit of
God markedly upon him, began to interpret. The messages
so frightened him that Celsio ran from the place, but outside
he recounted to others the strange sensation and understanding that had come to him in the chapel, and they persuaded
him to return. Now every time he tried to speak he choked up,
as though some invisible hand were trying to squeeze his
throat shut. Once again he fled the chapel.

Alexander continued to speak slowly in his new tongue,
repeating the words, knowing that Celsio was meant to
interpret them. But every time Celsio tried, the choking so
frightened him that he would flee the place again. Finally
someone suggested that he write the messages down, and as
he did the words began to flow, being dictated by the angel
and spoken by Alexander in tongues. One young day student
at the Institute (now a medical doctor) had been so scandal-
ised that he said it must be of the devil until he saw the first
written message, which he knew Celsio (with his lack of
education and literary ability) could never have made up.
These communications were a challenge from God to pray,

and indeed the Institute became a centre of prayer till the vacation time, when teams went out to preach the kingdom. It was the beginning of new stirrings of the Spirit across the land.

33 GOD TOLD HER TO STRIKE

Miller, himself a missionary, had arrived in Lavalle in the Andean foothills back in 1949, and soon came to the end of his spiritual tether. But after more than two months given to constant prayer, Miller felt the Lord was telling him to call the tiny local church to prayer: 'Go call the people to prayer – I will pour out my Spirit upon them. Tell them to come prepared to stay from 8 p.m. to midnight. If they are not prepared to stay the entire four hours, they must not come at all.' 'Could that really be the Lord?' he wondered to himself. The last time he had called the people for prayer like that no one had turned up. Then it had been at a convenient hour, but this would not be. However, the following Sunday he made the invitation to the little church group. Just before they started everything seemed discouraging – it was cold, the building was unheated, and there would be no transport after midnight. This all combined to make it doubtful whether anyone would respond, but besides his wife three others did come – one was a timid maid-servant and the other two were a backsliding Christian and his young wife.

The first night, after a time of meditation on the scriptures and much waiting upon God in silence, Miller asked if anyone had any impulse to say anything, to sing something or even to do anything at all. They all said no, except for the young wife, who confessed to a strong desire to get up and walk round the table and hit it! But she wouldn't do it. "It would be too foolish even to try it," she said. So the meeting ended.

The next night the same group assembled to seek the Lord again. It was almost an exact repetition of the previous night. During the four silent hours no one felt the slightest impulse to do anything for God except the young woman, who once again confessed to this same strange urge that she had had on the first night. But, as before, nothing would induce her actually to get up and strike the table. Once again the meeting seemed to end rather dismally. Could this really be the Lord? To give someone the desire to do such a thing as to rap the table? Was there anything like this in the Bible?

The third night the same three people joined Miller and his wife for another session of silent waiting upon God, and once again there was no response to any prompting of the Holy Spirit. When the time was nearly up, Miller asked the woman if she felt like rapping the table again. Once more she admitted that she did, but nothing would persuade her actually to do such a thing.

The Thursday night was a repeat performance of the first three nights – until 11 p.m., when Miller asked the young lady the same question. With a sense of shame, and somewhat reluctantly, she admitted that she still felt this strong urge to strike the table, but still she wouldn't do it. At this point Miller asked everyone to stand. Singing a chorus, he marched them round the table and encouraged each one to strike it. Finally the young lady reached out and hit the table.

Immediately a rushing wind swept through the room. Within seconds the timid maid-servant had her hands in the air, praising God in ecstasy – her face transformed and radiating joy. Meanwhile the backslidden man, who had consistently resisted God's call on his life, had fallen under the table and was beginning to pray in an unknown tongue. His wife, seeing what had happened, cried, 'Me too Lord?' just as the Spirit of God fell upon her also, and she too began to speak in tongues. Although they did not realise it at the time, the Holy Spirit was about to be poured out across Argentina in a new way.

34 TOMMY HICKS AND PRESIDENT PERON

In 1952 Tommy Hicks (then aged forty-four) was conducting
a series of meetings in California when God showed him a
vision. While he was praying a map of South America was
spread out clearly before him. The map appeared covered
with a vast field of golden wheat, bowed over and swaying in
the breeze, ripe for harvesting. As he looked, all the stalks
suddenly turned into human beings – men and women with
their hands raised in the air. They were calling to him:
'Come, Brother Hicks, come and help us.'

From this Macedonian call Hicks knew that God must
have something special for him to do in South America,
though he was still very ignorant about that part of the world.
As he prayed on he felt that God was giving him a message
which he scribbled down on the fly-leaf of his Bible: 'For two
summers will not pass over the earth until thou shalt go to
this land, for thou shalt not go by boat nor by land but as a
bird, flying through the air thou shalt go.'

Three months later, following an evangelistic crusade in
California, a pastor's wife stretched out her hand towards
Hicks in a prophetic prayer and, to his amazement, repeated
the identical message which he had already copied into his
Bible but which he had never mentioned to anyone.

As soon as he could, Tommy Hicks made arrangements to
travel to South America. Though he had very little money,
cash began to arrive by mail and he was now sufficiently
financed to buy a one-way ticket to Buenos Aires, with about
250 dollars to spare for his pocket. After some meetings in
Temuco, Chile, before the last leg of his flight, the word
'Peron' came into his mind, though he had no idea what this
meant except that he felt sure that God must be speaking to
him. He asked the air-stewardess if she knew what it meant.
'Yes,' she said, 'Peron is the President of Argentina!' Hicks
now knew that he was on course. He must see Peron.

The missionaries who met Tommy Hicks in Buenos Aires doubted whether any such high-level meeting could possibly be arranged, especially since the President of Panama was scheduled for a state visit at that time. Finally the persistent Hicks arrived at the office of the Minister of Religion, just as his secretary appeared limping across the room towards him. Almost before he knew what he was doing Hicks had started to pray for his healing, which came immediately. Seeing what had happened, the Minister of Religion promptly arranged an interview for him with the President himself.

When Hicks met Peron, the President was at that time suffering from eczema which so disfigured him that he allowed no photographs to be taken of himself. His ailment was common knowledge. Listening to Hicks telling what the Lord wanted to do in Argentina, Peron asked him: 'Can God heal me?' Hicks replied, 'Give me your hand.' Right there he prayed. Peron's skin was healed instantly. Stepping back in utter amazement, he wiped his hand across his face and exclaimed in astonishment: 'Dios mio, estoy curado! (My God, I am healed!).'

Peron soon gave instructions that Hicks should be supplied with whatever he needed – this included the use of a large sports stadium and free access to the state radio and press.

For fifty-two days Hicks preached to an aggregate attendance of about two hundred thousand, and the Pentecostal church in Argentina was launched into a period of very rapid church growth. The church historian Arno Enns described Hicks' campaign as 'a sovereign breakthrough by God'. Another influential study (W. Read *et al.*, *Latin American Church Growth*, p. 381) notes that 'many evangelicals in Argentina, whether or not they agreed with Hicks' theology, admit that his meetings broke the back of the rigid resistance in Argentina to the evangelical witness there'.

35 A HOLY HERMIT

In Benedicta Ward's *The Lives of the Desert Fathers* there is a
story of seven religious brothers who went to visit the hermit
John Thycopolis. The old man asked if anyone in the party
was a cleric. They all replied that none of them was. But one
in fact was a deacon, though he felt unworthy even to be
called a Christian and had only revealed his office confiden-
tially to one other member of the party, asking him to keep it
a secret. But nevertheless the old man pointed to him and
said, 'This one is a deacon,' and then admonished him kindly
for his deception.

36 WHAT GOD THOUGHT OF THEIR WORSHIP

A few years ago, as I reported in *Come, Holy Spirit*, I met the
pastor and his wife of a small but growing church in Hono-
lulu. This small free church group had been struggling on
one of the islands. The wife (a quiet person) felt so oppressed
by the Sunday services that she withdrew from the church for
a while to pray. Desperately she cried, 'What's wrong Lord?'
Then she could hardly believe what she sensed the Lord
telling her to do. Although she begged to be excused from
this, God seemed to be insisting. So she answered the Lord:
'Well, Lord, if my husband asks me to say anything when I
return,' (which she knew was most unlikely), 'I will do it.'

As she re-entered the building her husband spotted her
and called out: 'Have you anything for us from the Lord?'

Her heart sank, but she knew what she had to do. Nodding that she had, she went to the centre of the church, and with a hurried apology ('You all know me and know that I would never normally do anything like this'), she spat on the floor. 'That,' she cried, 'is what God thinks of our worship!' In that instant the Spirit of God fell upon the congregation in a most extraordinary way – the people slumped to the floor and wept in repentance. From that surge of new life the church was carried forward.

37   WHICH HOUSE TO VISIT

In the book *Ten New Churches* Roger Forster recounts the story of how one of the 'Ichthus' workers in South London was praying: 'Lord, we have a special outreach time on Sunday morning, but I have visited these tower blocks and houses so many times. Where do you want me to go today?' He received the words 'No. 8.' He went and found the place. A woman named Esme lived there, and when asked if she would like to come replied, 'Yes.' It was years since she had been to church.

The worker collected her the next Sunday and Esme wept all through the sermon. Roger went up to speak to her afterwards. 'Would Jesus come into my life?' she asked. 'Yes, of course,' said Roger. Then she added: 'And would he take away this pain from the surgical pin in my arm?' 'I am sure he wants to,' Roger replied. 'Come, let's ask him.' They prayed. Jesus came, and the pain had gone by that afternoon. Esme attended every meeting after that. Her next visit to the hospital resulted in the doctors leaving things untouched because she could now use her arm perfectly. On the second visit she was discharged without further treatment. After they had X-rayed her arm she heard them remark, 'We cannot find the pin!'

38 RECOGNITION IN A DANGEROUS PLACE

The well-known Dutchman, Brother Andrew, tells in his book *God's Smuggler* how after he was expelled from Yugoslavia for the second time he headed in his car, via Greece and Turkey, for Bulgaria. But he had no idea where to go when he got there, except that on his final night in Yugoslavia a Christian brother there had begged him to contact his closest friend in Sofia. In case this would prove to be possible, Brother Andrew memorised his name and address, not wanting it written down on his person in case it was later discovered in the course of a police check.

Once across the border into Bulgaria, Brother Andrew sat down on a hill-side and found himself actually surveying Sofia itself. He marvelled how God had used the very last person he had spoken to in one country to give him the first contact he needed in the next – in Sofia itself. He had problems finding the street on the only map in the hotel he could consult – and which the clerk grudgingly allowed him to glance at only briefly. He mentally noted the street he wanted – the only minor street included in the map, it seemed.

The next morning he left the hotel and headed immediately for Petroff's address. He found the street with no difficulty, just where the map had indicated. Now he only had to find the number. Obviously he had to avoid drawing any attention to himself, because this might indicate that Petroff was having a foreign visitor and create suspicion, and a neighbour might report him to the police.

As he walked along the pavement, a man came down the street from the opposite direction. They drew abreast, just as Andrew reached the number he was seeking. It was a large house; Andrew turned up the path, and so did the stranger. As they neared the front door, Andrew glanced for a fraction of a second into the face of the man who had arrived at the precise moment he had. And in that instant Andrew experienced one of the common miracles of the Christian life: 'Our spirits recognised each other. Without a word we marched side by side up the stairs. Other families lived in the house too: if I were making a mistake it would be very embarrassing. The stranger reached his apartment, took out his key, and threw the door open. Without invitation I walked into the house. Just as quickly he closed the door behind him. We stood facing each other in the darkness of the single room that was his home. "I am Andrew from Holland," I said in English. "And I," said the man, "am Petroff."'

After giving thanks to God together, not a minute of time was wasted. This was to reduce further any risks involved. 'I've heard', said Andrew, 'that both Bulgaria and Rumania are desperately short of Bibles. Is that true?' In reply Petroff led him to his desk. On the desk there was a typewriter with a sheet of paper in it, and next to that a Bible opened at Exodus. Petroff had been copying out pages from his Bible to complete another one. Andrew could hardly wait to show him the treasure he had waiting for him in his car. That night Andrew drove up to the apartment and, after checking the street first to make sure it was empty, proceeded to carry inside the first of many cartons of Bibles he was to deliver to this man over the years. Petroff was an ideal person to meet. He had Christian contacts all over Bulgaria, and he was able to distribute these Bibles to them. Often the secret churches they visited had only one Bible between them all.

39 A FOUR YEAR OLD BOY PREPARES TO DIE

In his book *Yet Not I*, the Anglican clergyman-cum-revivalist-cum-evangelist William Haslam, who was greatly used of God in England in Cornwall, Bath, East Anglia and London during the middle of the last century, tells a touching story about his four year old son, who appeared to be suffering very slightly from a fever (later believed to be scarlet fever).

One day he was allowed to get up and play in the nursery. He was happy but somewhat restless and kept asking for fresh flowers. These were procured for him, but though they were fresh and bright he was still not satisfied. Then he begged to be allowed to wear his white summer coat; this wish was also granted, but still he was not at rest. He asked his friend, Miss Hooper, to sing hymns to him, and sitting down in his white coat among the flowers, he looked up into her face and said: 'Doi'ee (his way of saying his own name, Georgy) 'is very ill, and getting worse.' He repeated this two or three times during the course of the afternoon.

The doctor was sent for, but he was detained until the evening, by which time it was clear that the little boy was dying. Miss Hooper asked him if he loved Jesus: 'Oh yes,' he replied, 'Jesus love me, and died for me; Doi'ee do love Jesus. Mamma, do not cry; Doi'ee is going to be with Jesus.' Soon after this he pointed upwards with his little hand, and looked up steadfastly as if he could see the Lord. Thus his spirit passed away, leaving a happy expression on his face. This all now seemed to explain to the grief-stricken family his restlessness and his request for bright flowers and the white coat.

40 A DREAM REVEALS THE HIDDEN LOCATION OF A WILL

In his book *Christianity and the Occult*, the late Canon John Stafford Wright, a highly respected principal of an Anglican theological college, and a man of clear evangelical persuasion, records the strange case of the Chaffin will, which he believed to be perfectly genuine.

Apparently James Chaffin had died in North Carolina in 1921. His only known will had been made out in 1905, and in this he had left all his property to his third son. The will was proven, but Chaffin's son died without heir about a year after inheriting.

In 1925 the second son had several visions of his father dressed in his old black overcoat. During one of these visions the father said: 'You will find my will in my overcoat pocket!' The eldest son still had the father's overcoat, and after a thorough search a paper was found in a sewn-up inner pocket. On it was written: 'Read the 27th Chapter of Genesis in my Daddie's old Bible.' The Bible was in a drawer, and tucked between the pages at Genesis 27 he found another will, dated 1919. In this will the father had divided his property equally between his four sons. Presumably this will was found to be genuine, for John Stafford Wright believed it to have been a spontaneous communication from Chaffin himself since no medium was involved. Equally it would appear to the present writer that this vision could have been a direct revelation from God.

41 A STUDENT IN PSYCHIATRIC CARE IS TOLD THE DURATION OF HIS STAY

John Sung was one of this century's most outstanding evangelists in the Far East. Leslie Lyall's biography of Sung contains the following story.

The Lord first came to Dr Sung on 10 February 1926. When breaking under the burden of his sin, Sung spent the night weeping in prayer. Suddenly he heard a voice saying to him: 'My son, your sin is forgiven.' At the time Sung was studying at Union Theological Seminary, a liberal academy in the United States. His tutors feared he was having a nervous breakdown, and he was put into a psychiatric ward for six weeks.

At the end of that time Sung was furious that he was not to be allowed to go back to seminary. In response to his outburst, Sung was transferred to a ward for violent patients. It was one of the worst experiences of his life. He asked the Lord what it all meant, and he was reminded that 'in all things God works for the good of those who love him' (Romans 8:28).

Then Sung received another personal message from the Lord: 'You must endure this treatment for 193 days. In this way you will learn to bear the cross and to walk the pathway of obedience to Golgotha.'

Sung was able to accept his situation, knowing now that it was all in the hands of the Lord. The psychiatrist allowed him to return to his original private room, where he had time to pray and to read the Bible (which altogether he read right through forty times). 'That was really my theological training,' he said later.

Sung had told no one during this period of enforced rest about the Lord's promised timing, but after exactly 193 days in the clinic he was in fact discharged.

This was sufficient proof to him that God had actually spoken to him and it was not his own imagination. The time in the clinic and the timing of his discharge were both significant factors in his future ministry. He died in his prime, but not before he had been used of God (becoming known far and wide as the John Wesley of his day) to shake the Church in China and South East Asia.

42   A CALLER FROM HAMILTON

Douglas McBain, in his book *Eyes That See*, records the following experience.

At a meeting in Scotland McBain was given a personal word for the daughter of a local Pentecostal pastor, who had told of his distress for his daughter Rosemary at a small prayer group for ministers. She was suffering from a deep depression following a bad bout of flu. The word which McBain was most surprised to be given for the minister to pass on to his daughter was simple and explicit: 'Tell Rosemary that a man will come from Hamilton and she must do whatever he tells her to do.'

Apparently later the same day a man from Hamilton did unexpectedly appear at the door of her home to see Rosemary. He was a consultant psychiatrist to whom the family GP had spoken earlier in the day. He prescribed some drug treatment which he assured her was all that was needed to put things right. To the surprise of all Rosemary accepted the treatment and was indeed soon perfectly well again. But for the prophetic word given her, she would hardly have taken the psychiatrist's advice because of the suspicion with which she regarded drugs of any kind.

43 THE VOICE ON THE STEREO

In his recent book *When the Spirit Comes with Power*, Dr John White has a chapter entitled 'Sandy: The Voice on the Stereo'. There he describes the experience of Sandy Solomon.

Sandy was a single thirty-seven year old woman. Her family was middle class, black and upwardly mobile. She had been raised a Methodist, and was baptised as an infant, but she had never understood what grace and the new birth are. Dr White describes her as a self-effacing, balanced woman with a healthy sense of humour. She was intelligent, perceptive and determined to succeed. She had become an assistant vice-president of a major national bank, with duties as a regional financial controller/planner.

On 26 December 1983, when Sandy was at home enjoying a record on her stereo equipment, she suddenly noticed what seemed like static drowning out the music. She could not understand this at all, though she thought it might perhaps have been caused by some sort of interference from the radio, but she had never noticed anything like it before. Then, with the music completely drowned out, the static suddenly stopped and in the silence Sandy heard a man's voice saying quite simply and clearly: 'Surrender to Jesus!' Just as suddenly the static returned and faded until the music came on again! (The whole incident lasted less than a minute, she thought.)

Sandy was frightened as she puzzled over how this could have got on to the recording. She replayed the record a number of times, but never again did she hear that voice. Slowly she realised the time had come for her to resolve her relationship with God, but she still delayed this for a number of days until, prompted again by an evangelistic programme on TV, she made her way across Los Angeles to the Vineyard Fellowship at Anaheim, where she 'accepted the Lord'.

For Sandy that was only the beginning of many strange encounters with God. In spite of some of the usual setbacks

and suffering Christians encounter, when John White last
met Sandy she was still serving the Lord in the power of the
Holy Spirit.

44   A VOICE IN THE NIGHT

One of many cases recorded by Kurt Koch in his *The Revival
in Indonesia* is that of Sarai, who on 29 September 1965 was
suddenly woken up in the night by the sound of a loud voice.
At first she was frightened and thought it must be a thunder
storm, but then she heard the words: 'Read Acts 2:2.' She got
her brother to do this for her, but as soon as he began she lost
consciousness. Then, while she was still apparently uncon-
scious, she heard a voice speak to her again and say: 'Read
Matthew 10:27–28!' Later she discovered that her family had
also heard these same words which had been spoken to her.

Then once more she heard a voice telling her: 'Go out and
preach the message I give to you.' This third command was
accompanied by a sense of heat upon her head which grew
increasingly intense, so that she cried out: 'Lord help me!'
The heat did not abate, however, and it continued to affect
her for some time, until finally she regained full consciousness. Sarai felt herself to be a new person – completely
changed.

She began preaching that same evening at about 6 p.m.,
and slowly a number of her neighbours and other villagers
gathered around her to hear what she had to say. Although
she had spent no time at all in preparation, she continued to
speak of things that the Lord had shown her until 3 a.m. the
following morning.

During her preaching she received further revelations

from God, telling the people of the fetishes they had in their houses and where they were hidden. Those convicted by her words hurried away to fetch their amulets and charms, bringing them back to the meeting and piling them up in a heap. Later that day the local church leader named Joseph arranged for them all to be burnt.

This eventful beginning was followed by another call from the Lord: 'Go out and preach!' he told her. 'But Lord I am an uneducated woman,' she protested. 'Read Matthew 10:20!' the Lord replied. There she found the words: '. . . for it will not be you speaking but the Spirit of your Father speaking through you.' Before setting out Sarai was shown the faces of the other people who were to accompany her – three young men and another Christian native woman. They agreed to go with her.

Just before her first preaching tour she was given a fresh vision – two messengers coming towards her in white who, after handing her a key, said to her: 'This key is the word of God, and with it you will be able to open the hearts of men.' Wherever the team now went, the words that Sarai spoke began to strike at the consciences of those who listened to her, compelling them to fetch out their fetishes and to burn them publicly. This was followed by an extraordinary ministry, with many people being healed. After labouring for some time on the island of Timor, Sarai sensed God calling her to go over to the neighbouring island of Rote to minister there.

She tried unsuccessfully to obtain a passage on a boat crossing over from Timor. Then she went down to the shore with her team and asked the Lord: 'How are we going to get across the sea?' The reply came: 'Wait another seven days, and I will send you a "prau" [a small sailing boat].' They waited, and, just as predicted, seven days later a prau arrived. The boat took them to Rote, where very soon the revival which had swept Timor was enveloping Rote also.

45   A VISION FOR A NATIVITY PLAY

Joan Jones of Harefield, Middlesex, wrote the following story
in an article for *Contact*, the church magazine of St Andrew's
Church, Chorleywood. We include it here because it is rather
different from any of the other stories.

Joan tells how she was awakened at 4.30 on a Saturday
morning in October 1988, and heard the words, 'Christmas!
Christmas!' sounding like a whispering echo. As she sat up it
stopped. Then, high on the wall just below the ceiling, a
miniature stage appeared (about 3ft by 2ft) with ladies in
long dresses and high pointed hats moving about on it. The
colours were magnificent, and she longed to awaken her
husband but could not take her eyes away from the scene
which gradually faded. This clearly conveyed to her the idea
of a play, and was followed by a commanding masculine
voice which said: 'The people will not go to the churches; you
must take the church to them. You are to have a Nativity on
the village green.' Joan was so sure that this was the Lord
that she kept praying: 'Please appear Lord!'

Joan continues: 'I then went downstairs and wrote a
Nativity. The readings, characters, carols, date and time just
seemed to flow. The site was to be the edge of the green near
the bus shelter. I thought this a strange place and wondered
about a better position!

'Later that morning, bursting to share my joy, I tele-
phoned my Christian friends and told them who they were to
be in the Nativity. Not one of them refused. Thinking about
the wise men I laughed as the obvious choice would be two
Christian GPs and my husband; they all agreed too.

'I visited the Church of England vicar of St Mary's and the
Roman Catholic priest of St Paul's. They were most co-
operative and promised to make it known in their churches
and to join us in person. The Baptist Hall was being dec-
orated; the Church of England Hall was already booked; but
the Roman Catholic Hall at the end of the High Street was

available to us for refreshments – soup, bread and mince pies. We would also be able to repeat our Nativity outside two pubs on the way there!

'Some pessimists said: "On the village green in December! What will you do if it rains?" "That's not my problem," I would reply, but in my daily prayers I asked the Lord for just one fine day with hot bright sunshine so that everyone could feel his presence with us.

'Two weeks after my vision I went to the theatre to see the musical *Kiss me Kate*, and there on the stage I was almost startled to see that one of the scenes recaptured my vision and seemed a wonderful confirmation from the Lord.

'I rang a farmer, whom I had never met, and asked to borrow one of his donkeys, and he promised to bring it along in his own horse box to the green, which he did.

'The Carols and Nativity programme started at 11 a.m. on 17 December. All the actors appeared in their costumes and gathered around the seat just where the Lord had indicated, next to the bus shelter. It was all just happening! We had a guitar and a flute. A crowd gathered as other people were standing waiting at the bus stop and yet others were simply passing by. All were able to see something of the real meaning of Christmas. As we sang "Light" the clouds opened and the warm bright sun streamed down. We looked up and said, "Thank you, Lord!"'

46 A MARRIAGE MADE IN HEAVEN

The Rev. Nicholas Rivett-Carnac, Bt., is the greatly loved and longstanding vicar (inducted in November 1972) of the well-known St Mark's Church, Kennington, whose parish church is only a cricket ball's throw from the Oval. At the age of forty-nine, Nicholas seemed set to remain a confirmed bachelor. But one day an old friend appeared for an unexpected chat, though obviously with something on his mind. After a while the friend looked Nicholas nervously in the eye and murmured hesitantly: 'Nicholas, I believe I have been given a word for you about marriage.' Nicholas went cold and simply replied, 'Oh?' But his friend continued more firmly: 'Yes, I believe I have been given the name of the person God is wanting you to marry!'

There was a longer pause. Nicholas was tired of people trying out their matchmaking schemes on him, but he braced himself and faced his friend whom he had known and trusted for many years. He could see that it was obviously not easy for his friend either. His friend continued: 'The name of the person I have been given by the Lord is Marigold Copeland.' Nicholas could hardly believe his ears, and the sense of delight which welled up within him, but he simply replied 'Oh!' again as his embarrassed friend slipped quietly away.

As the days went by Nicholas became increasingly taken up with the idea of having Marigold as his wife. He had known her since his first curacy days at Holy Trinity, Brompton, and had met her once since at a Fountain Trust meeting in the Central Hall, Westminster, where they sat together and shared a song sheet. It was at that meeting that he had first felt attracted to the thought of marrying her.

He went to consult his old college principal who had helped in this kind of situation in the past. He was surprised to find the suggestion greeted so positively by him. As his one-time principal pointed out: 'This comes simply as a confirmation of what you have already felt yourself.' Nicholas went away to pray, still mystified. There was no way he could see Marigold to try any soundings. When she had left him outside the Central Hall she had told him she was off to Africa, and who knew when she might be back from there?

Meanwhile Nicholas was actually struggling over the

ambiguity of his desires. On the one hand he very much liked the idea of marriage to Marigold, ten years his junior; on the other hand he was proud of his long bachelor years of independence, and he had unconsciously schooled himself in the three virtues of poverty, chastity and obedience. He finally came to the position before God of being willing to accept the responsibilities of marriage.

A few days later his old friend phoned. 'She's coming home in two days time. Would you like me to arrange a casual meeting?' he asked, and Nicholas found himself agreeing to the idea. This was the beginning of a friendship with Marigold.

Marigold had just come to a place of peace with God over her singleness, and now she was really confused about what God's will for her life could possibly be. Some months later, still perplexed, but liking the idea of marriage to Nicholas more and more, she was passing through Tunbridge Wells and found an open church there which she entered to spend time quietly in prayer. She simply poured out her heart to God and told him everything, praying that if this marriage was right then God would confirm it for her in some unmistakable way. No sooner had she prayed this than she felt a tap on her shoulder and looked up into the face of a man she did not know but whom she assumed must have been a member of that church. He spoke to her simply and directly: 'The Lord tells me I must tell you that whatever it is you are praying about and are burdened about, he wants you to know that it is all right. He wants you to go forward!' For Marigold this came as a perfect answer to her prayer; the complete confirmation that she had asked for. She and Nicholas were engaged at Christmas and married on 11 June 1977.

This, and other stories about Nicholas and Marigold Rivett-Carnac and St Mark's, Kennington, can be found in Jenny Cooke's book *Upon This Rock*.

47   DOES HE BELIEVE NOW?

At the Westminster Conference held in London in 1983 a
man approached one of the pastors among John Wimber's
team of counsellors. He said he could go along with just
about everything that John had said or done, except for the
'words of knowledge'. The pastor prayed in his spirit that he
would be shown the real reason that God had brought this
man to him so that he could help him. Suddenly a woman's
name came to mind. So he asked him, 'Does the name Rachel
mean anything to you?' Immediately the man became
embarrassed and confused. It did indeed! He confessed to a
past illicit sexual relationship with this woman which he
there and then repented of. This led to his forgiveness and to
peace with God. When the case was reported at a later team
meeting, one of the other counsellors casually enquired,
'Does he believe in words of knowledge now?' There was a
pause before the answer came: 'I don't know whether he does
or not, but I know *I* do!'

Part Two:
Counterfeit Revelations

48 TWISTING GUIDANCE

Believing that openness and honesty create the strongest possibility of genuine learning, we also include in this book frank disclosures of serious mistakes which have been made on the basis of supposed personal revelations from God.

Before proceeding further, however, let us look at the following amusing and not irrelevant story from Edmund Gosse's classic autobiography *Father and Son*, which was published at the beginning of this century.

Gosse Senior was a Victorian zoologist of some repute, but he was also a fervent member of an evangelical sect known to outsiders as the Plymouth Brethren. Throughout the biography we see how the boy learned to discover his own mind and eventually to escape from an environment dominated by doctrines which he was growing up to reject.

Anyone who has been brought up in such an environment will doubtless identify with the young Edmund. 'I remember on one occasion,' he writes, 'when the Browns, a family of Baptists who kept a large haberdashery shop in the neighbouring town (in Devon) asked for the pleasure of my company "to tea and games."' The Browns offered to fetch Edmund and bring him back home, but Gosse Senior was greatly perplexed, fearing that the company might be a little too worldly for his son.

'Father desired me to come up with him to the "boudoir" . . . that we might "bring the matter before the Lord". We did so kneeling side by side, with our backs to the window and our foreheads pressed upon the horsehair cover of the small, coffin-like sofa. My father prayed aloud with great fervour, that it might be revealed to me, by the Voice of God, whether it was or was not the Lord's will that I should attend the Brown's party . . . My father's attitude seemed hardly fair, since he did not scruple to remind the Deity of various objections to a life of pleasure and of the snakes that lie hidden in the grass of evening parties. It would have been more scrupulous I thought, to give no sort of hint of the kind of answer he desired or expected.

'. . . as I knelt, feeling very small beside the immense bulk of my father, there gushed through my veins like wine the determination to rebel . . . we rose presently from the sofa . . . and we faced one another in the dreary light. My father, perfectly confident in the success of what had really been a sort of incantation, asked me in a loud wheedling voice, "Well, and what is the answer which our Lord has vouchsafed?"

'I said nothing, and so my father, more sharply, continued, "We have asked him to direct you to a true knowledge of his will. We have desired him to let you know whether it is, or is not, in accordance with his wishes that you should accept this invitation from the Browns." He positively beamed down at me; he had no doubt of the reply . . .

'My answer came, in the high-piping accents of despair: "The Lord says I may go to the Browns." My father gazed at me in speechless horror. He was caught in his own trap, and though he was certain that the Lord had said nothing of the kind, there was no road open for him but just sheer retreat.'

The story illustrates how simple it is to manipulate others in the pretence of divine guidance. There is need for real spiritual and pastoral wisdom in handling this kind of situation.

Such wisdom begins with honesty, and it is for that reason that the following cases are included. We proceed now to demonstrate how pretence at 'divine revelations' has led to fraud, hypocrisy, manipulation and unnecessary distress in the following fourteen real-life situations.

49 DELIBERATE DECEIT

The writer was watching a TV programme in North America where the 'preacher' appeared to be given some amazingly detailed knowledge about individuals whom he had called out by their first name and surname from the crowded congregation.

When these people came up before the camera he would proceed to fill them in with further personal details such as the name of their spouse, if any, and the names and ages of their children, their doctor and a precise description of any particular health problem which was currently causing concern. The faith level of the people present was rising with each moment as the individuals involved gasped in astonishment at the preacher's knowledge concerning them.

When the word of healing was given in Jesus' name there was little surprise at the immediate success rate, which as far as one could possibly tell seemed to be quite genuine (and there is no good reason for not believing it still).

It was two or three years before a very sad secret was out. The 'preacher' had been in radio communication with an accomplice in a vehicle stationed outside the building; the accomplice had supplied accurate information from a questionnaire completed by volunteers in aid of research while queuing to enter the auditorium.

50 A DEMON THAT WASN'T THERE

The daughter of a well-known Christian leader was going through a rebellious stage at school. She was turned off church when she learned that the teacher in charge of the school Christian union had gathered the other girls to pray for her in her absence because the Christian teacher discerned she had a demon! The girl in question only learned of this 'discernment' at second hand.

51 A FALSE PROPHECY

The Rev. Dr James Packer, in his book *Keep in Step With the Spirit*, writes of his own experience: 'I think in this connection of the certainly sincere charismatic prophet who told me in 1979 that God had not brought me to Vancouver to write books, as I supposed, but to lead Christian people through a time of great internal division in the city churches. Well,' Packer commented in 1984, 'the churches seem much as they were in 1979, and here I sit writing this book!'

52 ANOTHER FALSE PROPHECY

An Anglican clergyman has recently shared with me his own distress caused by a false prophecy. While seeking God's will about his future, he was given a prophecy that God would soon be moving him to another parish. Earnestly desiring to be open to God about his life, he consulted his bishop. He agreed that it might well be right to be thinking of a move.

For the last two years the clergyman has had his name circulating the various patronage boards, but nothing suitable has been offered to him. He is now aged about sixty and feels that he must give up anticipating a move and concentrate on his parish, giving it everything he has got until he retires.

53 A MISGUIDED 'WORD'

In his book *The Healing Epidemic*, Peter Masters recounts the sad story of a childless couple who had managed to come to terms with their situation. Their case had been medically investigated and they had been informed that they could not have any children of their own. This was naturally a great disappointment to them.

Then one day a member of their Christian fellowship claimed to have a 'word of knowledge' for them that 'within twelve months they would have a child'. Eighteen months have since elapsed, and the couple are still childless. Their pastor has had to spend many hours counselling them. Their faith has been shattered.

54 TRAGIC DISASTER

Professor Verna Wright, in Peter Masters' book *The Healing Epidemic*, reports the tragic case of a couple from a church in Sheffield who had a child severely disabled with cystic fibrosis. (Cystic fibrosis is caused by a recessive gene, which means that it must be carried by two partners. If two such people marry there is a strong probability of the offspring having cystic fibrosis.) The couple went to the doctor to ask about a future family and the doctor advised against it, explaining that there was a one-in-four chance that any other children would be affected. They reconciled themselves to this situation.

One day a member of their church gave them a 'word of knowledge' and said: 'You will have a normal child!' The wife conceived and they had their baby. But it was more severely affected than the first, and for five years now they have been looking after a most disabled child.

55 IT ENDED IN SUICIDE

A female student in an English university joined the Christian fellowship there and became involved in a fruitful ministry helping others.

A young man came to visit her in order to encourage her with a 'prophecy'. He told her that the Lord had seen her good work and was very pleased with it. This was to be her life's work. It was not God's purpose for her to consider marriage.

The pronouncement was so traumatic that she fell into a deep depression which ended in her tragically taking her own life.

56 LOSS OF FAITH

A man from a reputedly 'live' church, which he attended with his family, had recently started his own business. He had built up an excellent staff and invested in a number of good programmes which were being advertised.

During the period of waiting for orders to come in, he went through a financial crisis. Should he cut back on the staff he would need urgently once the orders came in, or should he go deeper into debt?

Praying with some Christian friends, one of them professed to have a 'word of knowledge' that good news was in the post and would arrive in a white envelope. The businessman waited desperately for that letter, which never came, and ultimately he gave up on God and left the church.

57 A CASE OF CONFUSION

In response to a questionnaire, a friend wrote with commendable frankness and humility of a meeting at which a number of words of knowledge were given for 'barrenness'.

Any women present were encouraged to respond if this applied to them.

'I was in a ministry team and we were directed to pray for those who stood. I approached a lady who was standing near me and I started to pray for her. She began weeping.

'Having no insight, I asked her what she was feeling. "You do not understand," she said. "I have had a hysterectomy." Knowing that prayer did not exclude a miracle, I continued praying silently till she interrupted – "But I am not married." Now I knew that I had a problem! As we talked it became clear that she was rather a simple soul and that one of her main problems was that of loneliness. I therefore prayed for her that if the Lord had a partner for her she would be led to him, *etc.*

'A year later I was leading a mini-conference at the same venue and on the final night was chatting to a vicar who suddenly said, "I'd better go. I've brought along a lady tonight who is a little retarded and last year she was very upset, and our fellowship very put off, because some insensitive person prayed for her and promised her a baby even though she had neither a womb nor a husband. I must go and make sure she is OK."

'I had to own up to being that person, though slightly misquoted!'

58 THE LAST WORD ON THE SACRAMENTS!

In his book *Religion and the Decline of Magic*, Dr Keith Thomas gives two examples of people who believed that God had given them the last word on the sacraments, over which there were different opinions.

One lady asserted that she knew it was wrong to baptise infants because Christ had appeared to her personally to tell her so!

The other case was of a farmer's son from Shropshire who killed his mother and brother after quarrelling with them over whether the sacrament of Holy Communion should be received kneeling or not – apparently this too was a matter on which the farmer's son had recently received divine revelation!

59 TO WHAT GOOD PURPOSE?

John Wright, a member of a church team, cites the case of a lady he met abroad who came forward for prayer following a worship service in which the team had been involved.

This person, aged about sixty, asked him for prayer as she was feeling very confused and upset. She had been ill, and a group in her own church had been ministering to her. Since they were praying for her, she confessed to two middle-aged ladies in the group that years before, during the Second World War, she had given birth to an illegitimate baby daughter following an affair with a Canadian soldier.

This baby had been given the name Christine and was adopted at birth, and she had never seen her again. She believed the girl had been brought up in New Zealand, but she had never known anything more about her.

During the course of praying for her, the two middle-aged ladies both had dreams on the same night which seemed very similar. They proceeded to put two and two together and concluded that God had revealed to them a message for their sick friend. They proceeded to inform her starkly that they

had received a 'word of knowledge' to the effect that her
daughter Christine had committed suicide! Not unnaturally
this so-called 'revelation' had left the mother very grieved
and totally mystified as to what good there could possibly be
in such a distressing communication, with no apparent
means of confirming whether it was true or not.

60   SELF-DELUSION

Readers of Edmund Gosse's book *Father and Son* may remember the story he tells of a solicitor belonging to a Christian
sect who was accused of having executed a fraudulent will by
which he claimed sole inheritance of a rich client's property.

He not only admitted the fact in court, but he positively
gloried in it. 'He could be induced', wrote Gosse, 'to exhibit
no species of remorse, and, to the obvious anger of the judge
himself, stated that he had only done his duty as a Christian,
in preventing this wealth from coming into the hands of an
ungodly man, who would have spent it in the service of the
flesh and of the devil. Sternly reprimanded by the judge, he
made a final statement that at that very moment he was
conscious of his Lord's presence in the dock at his side,
whispering to him "Well done, thou good and faithful
servant"! In this frame of conscience, and with glowing
countenance, he was hurried away to penal servitude.'

61 ZAGREB: THE VIRGIN'S BLOOD

In his book *Serving Grace*, Michael Griffiths relates an experience which concerned him when he was present in a church in Zagreb, Yugoslavia, in September 1985. Apparently a woman stood up to say that the Lord had spoken to her and she wanted to share the word with the church. As she proceeded the congregation became very quiet, and Dr Griffiths' friend, who was interpreting for him, related what she had shared: 'She said that the Lord told her that more honour should be given to his mother Mary . . . that the blood he shed on the cross had all come from her, so that it was her blood which was shed . . .' Assuming that the interpreter had heard her correctly, that kind of statement is obviously open to serious criticism from both Catholic and Protestant Christians.

62 'PANICKY PROPHETS'

Michael Harper, writing in *Renewal* magazine in April 1974, under the caption 'Panicky Prophets', drew attention to some very misleading prophecies by leading 'charismatics'. David Wilkerson (whose book *The Cross and the Switchblade* has been a challenge and a blessing to so many) first shared a 'prophetic vision' at the Lutheran Charismatic Conference in Minneapolis in 1973, where among other things he declared that the 'honeymoon period' of the charismatic movement was over for the Roman Catholics and that persecution was coming from church leaders. He also moved into the field of economics, making statements about trade recessions, beginning in Germany, which would spread to the USA via Japan.

The prophecy was developed into a book. It drew a rebuttal from Ralph Martin, the editor of the Catholic charismatic magazine *New Covenant*, whose comment was that 'the emotional high-pressured conference talk and the current advertising campaign border on sensationalism'. Such methods appear to manipulate people's responses rather than allowing them the chance to apply biblical injunctions for testing such prophecy.

In the same article Michael Harper describes how Mother Basilea Schlink's community in Darmstadt, which has been a centre of renewal for thousands, had fallen into the same trap of sensationalism. The Mary Sisters had committed themselves to a newspaper production on the theme of the comet Kohoutek, which they saw as a warning of coming tribulation on this earth. In the event the comet sped harmlessly through the skies of 1973, unseen by the unaided human eye.

POSTSCRIPT:
THE NEED FOR DISCERNMENT

We Must Take These Mistakes as Warnings

The preceding fourteen accounts of mistaken claims to have received such revelations from God (pp. 73–84) serve as solemn warnings to us all. They illustrate how easy it is to deceive oneself and to manipulate others in the pretence of divine guidance. In some instances such outcomes were produced unconsciously, but in others they were deliberately intended. The twin dangers of self-deception and the deliberate deception of others are matters about which the church is not ignorant. But a simple response on the part of some people, in the light of such dangers, has been to ridicule *any* possibility of such divine revelation from God at all today.

C. S. Lewis, in his *Screwtape Letters*, once said that 'There are two equal and opposite errors into which our race can fall about . . . devils. One is to disbelieve in their existence. The other is to believe, and to feel an excessive and unhealthy interest in them.' We might say something similar to Christians today on the subject of claims to revelations from God: one is to disbelieve any such thing, while the other is to believe all such claims without exercising proper discernment.

The Need for Discernment

There have been times when God has spoken so dramatically, as in the many examples already cited, that there would usually be no doubt in our minds about it. The 'word' which we believe was from God came as a confirmation of other things that had been going on, so that when it finally came it was so clear we had no problem in recognising it.

When Nathan declared to David: 'You are the man,' it was an occasion when David's conscience was already working overtime regarding his adultery with Bathsheba and the murder of her husband, so that he could not fail at once to acknowledge that this was indeed from God. When the boy Samuel shared with Eli what Eli knew had been a call from God to Samuel the previous night, the old priest readily accepted the validity of it. When Saul of Tarsus heard the voice on the Damascus road the persecutor had good reason to know it was the Lord, even though he did not personally know him: 'Who are you *Lord*?' he asked.

The 'word', though it would seem to come as a 'one-off' communication, comes in fact as the culmination of a series of experiences – a troubled conscience perhaps or an unheeded call only subconsciously registered has preceded it. There are many such situations. The recipient knows it is God speaking. No problem!

But there are many other times when we experience niggling impulses. Sometimes these come after we have specifically sought the Lord over a particular matter, and sometimes after God has spoken spontaneously but faintly, not in the wind, nor in the earthquake, nor in the fire, but in a gentle whisper (1 Kings 19:12) – and even that was from behind (Isaiah 30:21), prompting us and urging us to obey what we sense God has been saying to us or telling us to say to others.

This is the area where we need help. It would be so satisfying and so satisfactory at this stage to be able to set out a fool-proof biblical check-list for anyone to apply at any time. Unfortunately it does not work like that. It is never so simple. We are only in a position to highlight some values to juggle with prayerfully in the process of trying to sift out the wheat from the chaff.

What is Discernment?

Some may be surprised to learn that there is no gift of discernment. What was once translated 'discerning of spirits' (AV) is now understood to mean 'distinguishing between spirits' (NIV); the basic gift required for a deliverance ministry (1 Corinthians 12:10). The gift could however have some part to play in discernment where it concerns the spirit of the speaker or the message spoken.

'Discernment', writes Thomas H. Green, SJ, in his *Openings to God* (Ave Maria Press, U.S.: 1987), 'is in popular terms, an art and not a science, that is, it is learned only by doing. Like any artist, the person skilled in discernment finds it difficult to formulate rules to teach another person how to discern well.'

A cyclist would find it hard to explain how he balances his weight on two thin tyres. He could not really tell how, except to say that 'practice makes perfect'.

Similarly, an experienced surgeon would probably find it impossible to explain simply to an 'intern' all the reasoning processes that lead to a successful diagnosis.

Likewise a valuer of paintings and antiques would find the same problem. There is a gift known in those circles as 'jizz' which instinctively conveys instant recognition of the indefinable. But it is mainly acquired over a period time by studying the history of art, *etc.*, and by practising alongside a recognised expert.

Discernment operates in a similar way through the Spirit. It becomes transrational. But it still needs exercising and training.

Since discernment is the art of interpreting God's word to us, God's will for us and God's truth about us, or something that concerns us or someone we come across, the essential is an experience of God – an awareness of his likes and dislikes, his desires for us and for the world.

Married couples acquire an instinctive sensitivity to the quiet word or small gesture which others may never notice. Young lovers don't possess it. Beginners in prayer don't normally possess it about God either, but as the relationship with God develops so does our instinctive judgement about what pleases him. There is no short cut to acquiring the art. But it does help to know the main values which we need to bear in mind.

The Values Involved in Discernment

The Character of the Prophet

As Jesus said: 'No good tree bears bad fruit, nor does a bad tree bear good fruit. Each tree is recognised by its own fruit. People do not pick figs from thornbushes, or grapes from briers' (Luke 6:43–44). What counts is not spiritual experiences or extraordinary gifts, but the way a person lives. The more mature, stable, virtuous and godly a person is, the more we can rely upon that person to exercise the gifts of the Spirit with maturity, purity and power.

Although the character of the person with the revelation is one good rule-of-thumb method, it is still not fool-proof. There are even some exceptions to this rule in the Bible:

1 Balaam was given a glorious prophecy concerning Christ: 'A star will come out of Jacob; a sceptre will rise out of Israel' (Numbers 24:17) – but he abused his office for profit (Jude 11).
2 Jesus charged the scribes and Pharisees with hypocrisy, and yet he told the people to obey them: 'The teachers of the law [the scribes] and the Pharisees sit in Moses' seat. So you must obey them and do everything they tell you' (Matthew 23:2–3).
3 The high priest Caiaphas, who was wicked, and was one of those responsible for putting Christ to death, prophesied truly: 'You do not realise that it is better for you that one man die for the people than that the whole nation perish' (John 11:50; 18:14).

So there may be the odd occasion when a person whose reputation might not be too good does in fact have a word from the Lord.

Unknown prophets should be avoided, though scripture suggests there will always be some who will seek them out: 'To suit their own desires, they will gather around them a great number of teachers to say what their itching ears want to hear' (2 Timothy 4:3b). Some will go miles to find a 'spiritual' teacher they are sure will give them the advice they want to hear.

Anyone looking for an architect or a building contractor would surely look for a man with a solid reputation for honesty and good work. Anyone hiring a new man would undoubtedly be careful to check his credentials and keep an eye on his work. This simple common sense applies to all 'revelators' (spiritually gifted people), seers and prophets, even though they may speak eloquently and profoundly and most spiritually.

The Spirit of the Prophet

John gives us a *recognition* test: 'This is how you can recognise . . .' (1 John 4:2). Question: Does he believe that Jesus Christ has come in the flesh (1 John 4:2–3)? Ask him!

Paul gives us a *religious* test: 'No-one who is speaking by the Spirit of God says . . .' (1 Corinthians 12:3). Question: Does he confess that Jesus Christ is Lord (1 Corinthians 12:3)? If in doubt ask him!

Then there is a *relationship* test. Question: Does he know the Lord? Has he been 'born again' (John 3:5, 7)? Every true Christian should be in such a relationship with the Lord that he knows his voice (John 10:2–5). A good analogy would be the experience of human love. When two people love each other, each becomes expert in interpreting the moods, the wishes, the hopes and the fears of the other. A wife goes into a tailor's shop to buy a tie for her husband. She quickly inspects the range on view. 'Instinctively' she says: 'No, he would not like that one . . . Not that one either . . . Nor this . . . Ah, yes! This is the one he would like.' How does she know? She develops her gift of discerning her husband's tastes over years of living together and common sharing day by day. Probably in the early days she often got it wrong — bringing home something he did not like and would not wear!

Finally there is a *resonance* test. Question: Is there an inner witness within us to confirm it? This latter is a simple principle which Bruce Yocum calls 'resonance'. He goes on to explain how objects have certain characteristic frequencies at which they vibrate near another vibrating object with the same characteristic frequency (another wine glass of the same size and weight and shape); the second object will begin to vibrate by itself. That is something like what happens when we hear the voice of the Lord.

The first way we know we have a witness in our own hearts and spirits about a revelation is through a peaceful assurance about its rightness. If it is right it will not grate or repel so long as we ourselves are in true fellowship with God and are walking in the light with our brothers and sisters in Christ.

There is an important proviso here. Many times as individuals we will not feel any real spiritual response to a revelation — either positively or negatively. That is not unusual. It does not necessarily invalidate the revelation, nor does it indicate that there must be something wrong with us. But again others may experience some 'spiritual response' to a revelation from God. That response, though not definitive proof in itself, can help us to determine further whether a revelation is from the Lord or not.

The second witness will be to the revelation's spiritual tone and effect. Firstly there will be a sense of moving in the flow of what God is already doing. When, for example, a church has started to build after months of praying and planning, a 'word' to pull it all down is hardly in the flow of what a responsible group have sensed God to be doing. Secondly it will also be in harmony with God's Spirit. Revelation which is frightening, harsh, condemning or critical seldom comes from the Holy Spirit.

The third witness is to whether the 'word' leads into freedom or bondage. Many cult leaders have built up a following of people who have never stopped to weigh up what was actually happening to them. They have not discerned that they themselves were moving step by step into bondage through a leader who needed to substantiate his authority by a claim to divine revelations. That is how the tragic mass suicides of some nine hundred members of The People's Temple cult in Jonestown, Guyana, came about as recently as ten years ago. Jim Jones' disciples were so glad to find a leader who would take responsibility for all their decisions in their morally confused world that they relaxed their personal common-sense discernment and sacrificed their inner integrity to his treacherous leadership.

The fourth witness is to whether what the 'word' leads into will glorify the Lord Jesus.

The Result of the Message

Does what is predicted come to pass (Deuteronomy 18:21–22)?

There are several provisos here.

First, it usually takes time to show whether a revelation has come to pass. And sometimes the revelation may be a warning from God of some impending disaster. It does not help if it is not believed till the disaster we were warned against has to fall upon us. Such warnings are to help save us from disaster. Examples in this book are the flood story (p. 43) and the aircrash premonition (p. 42).

Second, sometimes blessings predicted are conditional. If the conditions are not met then the blessing will not be granted. Judgements are also predicted unless there is repentance (*e.g.* Jonah 3:4–5, 10). Jonah was upset with God because the people of Nineveh repented after his prophecy and the disaster of God's judgement was averted. He felt his credibility as a genuine prophet of the Lord was open to question.

Third, it has been known for people to misinterpret a revelation so that it may appear that it has not come to pass when in fact it has. Sometimes we hear only what we have wanted to hear.

Fourth, even when the prophet predicts something that actually comes to pass, he still may not be a trustworthy prophet. He could still lead into error (Deuteronomy 13:1–3).

The Content of the Message

The first question we must ask ourselves is: 'Is it in line with Christian teaching?' Paul said that no new revelation could ever supersede the original gospel – not even if he himself, or even an angel from heaven, brought it (Galatians 1:8–9). Nothing which contradicts plain Christian teaching (clearly summarised in the creeds) can be admitted as true revelation from God. Remember when seeking to understand the Bible that the plain thing is the main thing, and the main thing is the plain thing! This is a very good rule of thumb.

Scripture must be the criterion against which all other revelation is measured (*cf.* 1 Corinthians 15:13–19). In her book *How to Test?* (N. Florida: Roxanne Brant Ministries, 1981), Roxanne Brant suggests that when we ask the question, 'Is it scriptural?' we have to consider five basic questions:

1 Is there any adulteration of scripture?
2 Is there any addition to scripture? The verse giving the warning against this is found in Revelation 22:18. It applies specifically to the book of Revelation, but the principle holds for the whole Bible. This is our problem with the prophecies of Joseph Smith. His *Book of Mormon* is adding to the Bible in such a way that it undermines some of the plain teaching of the Bible.

3   Is there any subtraction from scripture? Revelation
    22:19, which refers to this, again applies particularly to
    the book of Revelation, but the principle applies to the
    whole Bible. Here we cite the example of Mary Baker
    Eddy, the founder of Christian Science, whose teaching
    plainly detracts from scripture.

4   Is there any mixture of man's ideas with God's truth?
    Paul warns against this: 'Do not let anyone who delights
    in false humility and the worship of angels disqualify you
    for the prize. Such a person goes into great detail about
    what he has seen, and his unspiritual mind puffs him up
    with idle notions' (Colossians 2:18). Some brethren are
    tempted to project their wishful thinking in the pretence
    of a revelation from God. Others have been known to get
    chips off the shoulder under the same guise.

5   Is the message balanced or unbalanced? Let us beware of
    all hobby-horse syndromes.

Does it Bear Good Fruit?

This has rather similar difficulties in application to the
question about whether the prediction comes to pass or not.
The problem is that fruit takes time to mature. But good gifts
are like good fruit trees, and will bear good fruit.

However it is also the case that true prophecy can legiti-
mately cause strife, anger and violence. This was so with the
Old Testament prophecies of Elijah and Jeremiah, and was
certainly the case with Jesus. He even said he had not come to
bring peace but a sword in some situations where people
would not receive him (Matthew 10:34; *cf.* Luke 12:52–53).

Discernment in Receiving Revelations

We envisage three separate situations here:

1   When it is believed that a revelation has come direct from
    God to oneself for oneself.

2   When it is believed one has a revelation from God for
    another person or the church.
3   When it is claimed that it has come from God via others
    for oneself.

Clearly in all these situations it is always good to follow the
prudent example of Jesus' mother, Mary, who upon hearing
predictions concerning her son and her personal suffering
that would be involved with his 'pondered these things in her
heart' (Luke 2:19).

There are times when we think God may be speaking
things to us that we can share publicly, knowing that if we are
wrong there are others to check it, counter it, correct it, *etc.* If
we are wrong, provided we have tried to keep within the
prescribed parameters (of 1 Corinthians 14:3, 24, 31), there
will be no harm done. Even in doubt we may be right, and the
word spoken out may be just the very word to confirm for
someone what God is already saying in other ways.

But there are other 'words' which could clearly have
momentous potential for harm if they were acted upon in
blind faith. Such 'words' require proper and distinct confirmation by God in other ways, and preferably consultation
with the leadership of the local church first before being
shared or followed.

It is worth noting the wise and helpful advice once given by
Jean Darnall (quoted in Joyce Huggett, *Listening to God*
(London: Hodder & Stoughton, 1986), p. 141), who said: 'If
you believe God has told you to do something ask him to
confirm it to you three times: through his word, through
circumstances, and through other people who may know
nothing of the situation.'

The writer was recently with a pastor from Kansas City, in
the USA, and this man told how one night he had an
extraordinary dream when the angel of the Lord came to him
and told him he wanted him to do something which was quite
unusual for him. While he was pondering this strange dream
a man who claimed to be a prophet of the Lord, whom he had
only recently come to know, approached him and said: 'Well,

what did you think about the Lord's visitation the other night?' Our friend did not give an inch. 'When was that?' he fenced. 'On Thursday night,' the man replied. 'What are you talking about?' the pastor fenced again. 'Well,' said the prophet, 'are you going to tell me or have I got to tell you? Because you are such a hard man and won't believe me, I will have to tell you.' The prophet proceeded to tell him exactly how the angel of the Lord had come to the pastor in his dream and precisely what he had said!

Our confirmations may not come as dramatically as that, but if we pray, watching and waiting patiently, some kind of confirmation will come. Timothy Pain shares a delightful story in his little 'Ashburnham Insights' book *Prophecy*, where he describes a major hiccup in his courtship days with his wife Alison. They had first met in 1971, but had separated after a couple of years because of continuous rows. They met up again in 1975, with some good reason for believing that their relationship would now be much better, and they became engaged to be married soon after.

By the following spring they were back in their 'old cycle of rows and reconciliations' and were seriously thinking of breaking off their engagement. One morning, during the course of his daily Bible readings, Tim was suddenly struck by a feature in Matthew's narrative of the birth of Christ that indicated how clearly God had guided through dreams. It was a new thought to him that God could guide him too through a dream. He said that when he went to bed that night he was so convinced that God was going to speak to him through a dream that he stayed awake all night waiting for it!

While visiting his fiancée the next morning, the telephone suddenly rang and a friend, a lapsed Christian whom they had not seen for a couple of years, rang to tell Alison about a dream she had just had concerning both Tim and Alison!

In her dream this friend had watched them repeatedly climbing up a slippery mountain, seeming to take three steps up and slipping back two, before they eventually made it to the top. Their friend seemed very amused by such a funny

dream, but Tim was awestruck. They felt encouraged by
this to press on to marriage. 'Ten years later,' wrote Tim,
'it is still three steps up and two back, but we're making
progress.'

These were extraordinary confirmations from God. We
may find that some confirmations are not quite so extraordinary, but are nevertheless significant.

In 1969 we were home on leave in the UK after having
sought to serve the Lord for ten years in Chile and feeling it
was time to look for a position in England. There was a lot of
pressure put on us to go back, but we prayed that if it really
was right the Lord himself would guide us clearly. I was in
church one Sunday morning, having left Mary at home with
the four small girls. During the reading of the first lesson my
mind was wandering over the sermon I was about to preach
when suddenly I *knew* that we had to go back to Chile.

I was not at that moment consciously preoccupied about
returning; I was simply thinking about my sermon! I did not
know how I knew, or even what I had heard to make me
so sure now. I thought it must have had something to do
with the lesson. As I glanced back over the reading (from
the AV), one line in it jumped out at me: 'For thus saith the
Lord God ... "In returning and rest shall ye be saved"'
(Isaiah 30:15). That then was what I had heard so distinctly,
I thought.

But I wondered, 'Could that really have been the Lord?
After all, it was simply part of the lesson which had been
read.' Though I had a strong feeling that it was God's call,
such a major volte-face for us would still need to be clearly
confirmed of course.

My wife Mary was not at all keen at that time about going
back. Other things apart, we had had many problems with
the children's health in Chile and I wondered how I was now
going to share this news, which quite honestly I had never
expected to bring to her. I prayed all the way home and was
flabbergasted to be greeted by Mary, who was bursting to tell
me how the Lord had spoken to her that morning in her
prayer time, during my absence, about going back to Chile!

Here was an unwanted(!) call from God, both unexpectedly given and independently confirmed. With hindsight we see how that call proved to be a turning-point both in our personal lives and our separate ministries.

Discernment in Communicating Revelations

In the exercise of all the gifts, it is important to know that none of us is infallible and that even though we may have often been right in the past we could still be wrong next time! This calls for great humility of spirit, and often for courage, because no one likes to be wrong. It would be catastrophic indeed to mislead another person into taking a major decision – possibly affecting both his life and that of his family – when one was being misled oneself. We have seen tragic examples of this in the cases cited earlier.

For any effective ministry in the exercise of discernment in the individual Christian or in a local church, there are some vital governing factors which must be taken into account.

First, the person needs to have the assurance that he has been born again by the Holy Spirit of God (John 3:5, 7), and that he knows Jesus Christ as his Saviour and his Lord.

Second, he needs to want to grow into maturity, which means he desires to learn about Christian discipleship and practise it at all costs. We are not to be hearers of the word only, but doers also (James 1:22).

Third, he will be a man of prayer who both reads his Bible and worships regularly with the Lord's people.

Fourth, he will need to have some experience of the Holy Spirit's anointing on his life.

Fifth, he will deliberately seek to cultivate the fruits of the Spirit (Galatians 5:22–23), which are all summed up in the one word 'love'. This will always include putting oneself in the other person's place and doing to others as one would be done by! It is important to pray about the best way of communicating a revelation from God.

Sixth, he will bear in mind the example of Jesus himself, who:

1 He only said and did *what* he heard and saw the Father saying and doing (John 5:19).
2 He only said what the Father said, and only said it *how* the Father wanted him to say it (John 12:49). There are counter-productive ways of saying what we sense God is saying. Paul, on the other hand, talks about 'speaking the truth in love' (Ephesians 4:15).
3 He only said and did things *when* the Father told him, and not before (John 16:12). Even though Mary was his mother, Jesus objected to her urgent appeal for instant intervention at the wedding at Cana in Galilee (John 2:3–4), and delayed after the pressing plea of his two friends Martha and Mary at the time of Lazarus' terminal illness (John 11:3–6), because the time was not right.
4 Sometimes, maybe, he was shown things that he never got round to telling the persons concerned at all (John 16:12). Such revelations need not necessarily be communicated, but may serve as a spur to prayer or a guide for ministry.

We remember one time when a woman came forward for prayer and it was 'impressed' upon my wife that she had been molested by her father as a girl. Obviously it would have been quite out of place to suggest such a thing (especially when one could be wrong), so my wife asked the Lord for wisdom to know what she was meant to do with this 'knowledge'.

She immediately got the impression, which she believed came from God, that she was to pray into the woman's relationship with her father. So she asked her if she would be happy about that. The woman nodded her agreement. No sooner had Mary invited the Holy Spirit to come into the relationship between this woman and her father than the woman broke down, and out came the whole story. Mary was then able to minister healing into an area which the Lord had so clearly indicated.

How Do We Get Discernment?

Strictly speaking, as we have seen, discernment is not a gift of the Spirit mentioned in any of the New Testament lists, although there is a gift of 'distinguishing between spirits' (1 Corinthians 12:10) and there are the gifts of 'the message of knowledge' and 'the message of wisdom' (1 Corinthians 12:8). All these are ingredients of discernment. James encourages us to ask God for any good gift (James 4:2). We might conceivably feel it is also right to request someone who evidently has discernment to impart it to us on the basis of verses like Romans 1:11 (Paul says: 'I long to see you so that I may impart to you some spiritual gift') and 2 Timothy 1:6 (Paul says: 'Fan into flame the gift of God, which is in you through the laying on of my hands'). At the same time, however, those who have gifts should not lay hands suddenly on someone to impart gifts to them (1 Timothy 5:22).

It is helpful too to find people with the spiritual gifts we covet and to get alongside them as Elisha did with Elijah. What is more, the mantle of Elijah eventually came to rest upon Elisha with a double portion of his gift (2 Kings 2:9): let us be encouraged by this.

Once we have found people with the anointing, we can try to work with them as much as possible in ministry. Just watch them; learn to see what they see. In the process it seems that initially the revelatory gifts are imparted to us (sort of wear off on us) in embryonic form. Careful and constant use will enhance their effectiveness.

WORKS MENTIONED IN THE TEXT

Brother Andrew, *God's Smuggler* (London: Hodder & Stoughton, 1967)

Rosemary Attlee, *William's Story* (Crowborough: Highland Books, 1987)

Roxanne Brant, *How to Test?* (N. Florida: Roxanne Brant Ministries, 1981)

George Canty, *The Practice of Pentecost* (Basingstoke: Marshall Pickering, 1987)

Jenny Cooke, *Upon This Rock* (London: Hodder & Stoughton, 1989)

Mita Edwards and Mark Buntain, *Miracle in the Mirror* (Newton Abbott: Torbay Publishing, 1982)

Christian Lalive d'Epinay, *Haven of the Masses: A Study of the Pentecostal Movement in Chile* (London: Lutterworth Press, 1966)

Eifion Evans, *The Welsh Revival of 1904* (Brytirion, Bridgend: Evangelical Press of Wales, 1974)

Roger Forster (ed.), *Ten New Churches* (Bromley: MARC Europe, 1986)

Rex Gardner, *Healing Miracles: A Doctor Investigates* (London: Darton, Longman & Todd, 1986)

John Goldingay (ed.), *Signs, Wonders and Healing* (Leicester: Inter-Varsity Press, 1989)

Edmund Gosse, *Father and Son* (1907) (Harmondsworth: Penguin Books, 1983)

Thomas H. Green, *Openings to God* (Ave Maria Press: U.S., 1987)

Michael Griffiths, *Serving Grace* (Bromley: MARC Europe, 1986)

Wayne Grudem, *The Gift of Prophecy* (Eastbourne: Kingsway Publications, 1988)

William Haslam, *Yet Not I* (London: Morgan & Scott, *c.* 1879)

Clifford Hill, *Towards the Dawn* (London: Collins Fount, 1980)

Harold Hill, *How to Live Like a King's Kid* (Plainfield, NJ: Logos International, 1974)

Joyce Huggett, *Listening to God* (London: Hodder & Stoughton, 1986)

Munro Kerr, *Operative Obstetrics*, ed. P. R. Myerscough (London: Baillière, Tindall & Cox, 1981)

J. B. A. Kessler, Jr, *A Study of the Older Protestant Missions and Churches in Peru and Chile* (Goes, Holland: Oosterbaan & le Cointre N.V., 1967)

Kurt Koch, *The Revival in Indonesia* (Berghausen, 7501 Berghausen Bd., Western Germany: Evangelization Publishers, c.1970)

C. S. Lewis, *The Screwtape Letters* (1942) (London: Collins Fount, 1981)

David C. Lewis, *Healing: Fiction, Fantasy or Fact?* (London: Hodder & Stoughton, 1989)

Leslie Lyall, *John Sung* (London: CIM, 1954)

George Mallone, *Those Controversial Gifts* (London: Hodder & Stoughton, 1983)

Catherine Marshall, *Something More* (London: Hodder & Stoughton, 1977)

Peter Masters, *The Healing Epidemic* (London: The Wakeman Trust, 1988)

Douglas McBain, *Eyes That See* (Basingstoke: Marshall Pickering, 1986)

Briege McKenna, *Miracles Do Happen* (Dublin: Veritas Publications, 1987)

R. E. Miller, *Cry For Me Argentina* (Brentwood: Sharon Publications, 1988)

J. I. Packer, *Keep in Step With the Spirit* (Leicester: IVP, 1984)

Timothy Pain, *Prophecy*, Ashburnham Insights (Eastbourne: Kingsway Publications, 1986)

Jackie Pullinger and Andrew Quicke, *Chasing the Dragon* (London: Hodder & Stoughton, 1980)

David Pytches, *Come, Holy Spirit* (London: Hodder & Stoughton, 1985)

W. Read, V. Monterosso, H. Johnson, *Latin American Church Growth* (Grand Rapids, Michigan: Wm B. Eerdmans, 1969)

Demos Shakarian, *The Happiest People on Earth* (London: Hodder & Stoughton, 1977)

C. H. Spurgeon, *Autobiography: The Early Years* (Edinburgh: The Banner of Truth, 1967)

Keith Thomas, *Religion and the Decline of Magic* (Harmondsworth: Penguin Books, 1973)

Ignacio Vergara, SJ, *El Protesantismo en Chile* (Santiago: Editorial del Pacifico, 1962)

c. Peter Wagner, *Signs and Wonders Today* (Almonte Springs: Creation House, 1987)

Peter Wagner, *The Third Wave of the Holy Spirit* (Ann Arbor: Servant Publications, 1988)

Benedicta Ward (ed.), *The Lives of the Desert Fathers*, trans. N. Russell (Oxford: Mowbray, 1981)

John White, *The Cost of Commitment* (Leicester: IVP, 1976)

John White, *When the Spirit Comes with Power* (London: Hodder & Stoughton, 1989)

David Wilkerson, *The Cross and the Switchblade* (Marshall Pickering: Lakeland Paperbacks, 1964)

John Wimber, *Power Evangelism* (London: Hodder & Stoughton, 1985)

John Wimber and Kevin Springer (eds), *Riding the Third Wave* (Basingstoke: Marshall Pickering, 1987)

John Stafford Wright, *Christianity and the Occult* (London: Scripture Union, 1972)

Nigel Wright, *The Fair Face of Evil* (Basingstoke: Marshall Pickering, 1989)

Bruce Yocum, *Prophecy: Exercising the Prophetic Gifts of the Spirit Today* (Michigan: Servant Publications, 1976)